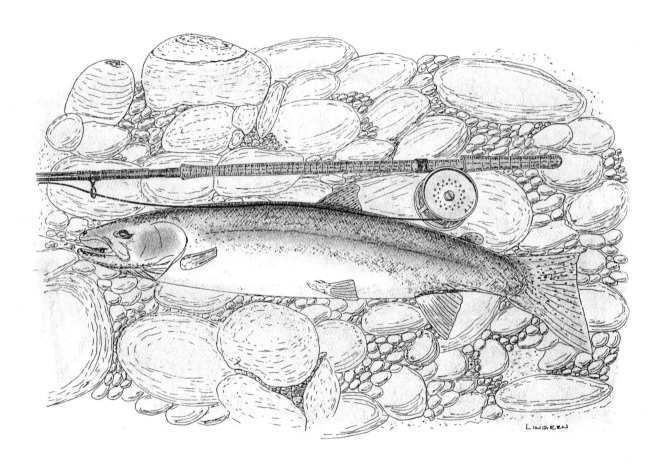

Thompson River

Thompson River

Arthur J. Lingren

Frank Amato
PORTLAND

River Journal

Volume 2, Number 3, 1994

Borrowing time from fly fishing to research the history of the sport in British Columbia, Art Lingren shows a remarkable degree of proficiency in both arenas. There is probably no one who can wield the fly rod better or tie more effective flies for steelhead than Art. But his interests go deeper than that. In British Columbia, he is to fly fishing what Ben Crenshaw is to golf—the sport's dedicated historian. Acknowledging that dedication, the newsletter of the B.C. Federation of Fly Fishers named him their official historian.

Writing about history and steelhead fishing on the Thompson River came naturally to Art. He has fished the river for twenty-five years, beginning as a lure angler and graduating to the fly fifteen years ago. He knows the river expertly, where and when to fish on varying water levels and with his two-handed rod can fire a fly into the most distant steelhead holds. His account of this magnificent river and its severely depressed steelhead stocks is, to those who love and fear for both, a welcome addition to British Columbia's angling literature.

Art Lingren lives in Vancouver as he has all his life with his wife, Beverley and his son, Charles. He is Supervisor of Engineering Services with the Greater Vancouver Regional District, which grants him generous leave for his excursions to British Columbia's great rivers.

Van Egan, Campbell River, B.C.
November 1993

◆

Acknowledgments

Thanks to those who willingly lent a helping hand: Lee Straight, Brent Lister, Ian McGregor, Dr. W. E. Ricker, Bob Hooton, Bob Taylor, Jerry Wintle, Dave Winters, Peter McVey, Ron Schiefke, Ron Grantham, Van Egan, Peter Blain and Ehor Boyanowsky.

◆

Series Editor: Frank Amato

Subscriptions:
Softbound: $30.00 for one year (four issues)
$55.00 for two years
Hardbound Limited Editions: $80.00 one year, $150.00 for two years
Frank Amato Publications, Inc. • P.O. Box 82112 • Portland, Oregon 97282 • (503) 653-8108

Design: Joyce Herbst
Photography: Art Lingren
Cover Photo: Brian Chan • Map: Tony Amato
Printed in Hong Kong
Softbound ISBN:1-878175-47-5, Hardbound ISBN:1-878175-48-3
(Hardbound Edition Limited to 500 Copies)

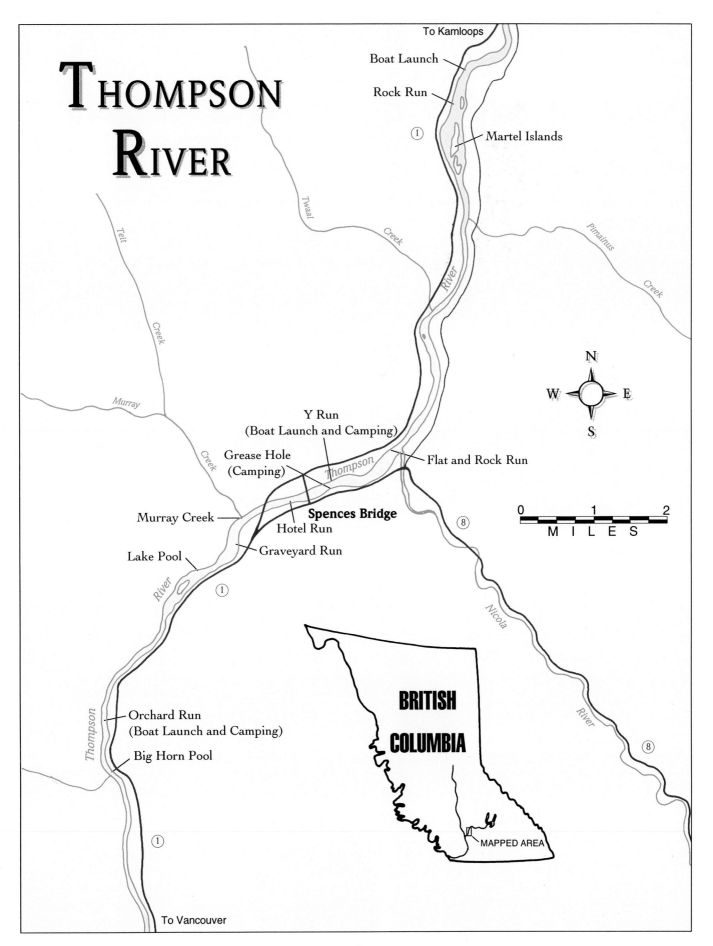

THOMPSON RIVER

To Kamloops

Boat Launch

Rock Run

Martel Islands

Twaal Creek

River

Pimainus Creek

Teit Creek

Murray Creek

N
W   E
S

Y Run
(Boat Launch and Camping)

Grease Hole
(Camping)

Thompson

Flat and Rock Run

Murray Creek

Spences Bridge

Hotel Run

Graveyard Run

Lake Pool

0   1   2
M I L E S

Nicola

River

Orchard Run
(Boat Launch and Camping)

Big Horn Pool

Thompson

BRITISH COLUMBIA

MAPPED AREA

River

To Vancouver

*Kamloops fishermen working the south Thompson River, 1902. L to R; Dan Koughan, Harry Campbell, Walter Tarrant, Fred Burns and Arthur Lauder.
Photo courtesy of Kamloops Museum & Archives.*

THOMPSON RIVER

◆

*T*HERE ARE RIVERS AND THERE ARE RIVERS AND THERE are steelhead and there are steelhead. When the two—rivers and steelhead—unite, you have the most exciting fishing on earth. Steelhead and rivers go together but it takes the right combination of river and fish before that truly exceptional fishery exists.

Most steelhead fishermen know that steelhead range in size from about 3 pounds (1.4 kilograms) to over 30 pounds (14 kilograms). Some rivers have steelhead of small average size and some have steelhead of large average size. Some steelhead run up short, coastal, low-gradient rivers, whereas others travel a couple of hundred miles and more into inland drainages, often through turbulent, high-velocity sections of water that the fish can pass only at certain times of year.

Over the past twenty-five years of wandering, I have sampled close to three dozen steelhead rivers and caught steelhead from most of them. Only one has drawn me back year after year. This river, which is home to sleek "marathoners," is large and the fish have plenty of room to show their mettle when hooked. That river is the mighty Thompson. The Thompson steelhead are a race of superb, large-average-sized, summer-run fish. The leaders of the Thompson River stocks show up in the Spences Bridge fly fishing area in late September and the bulk of the run arrives in October and November. The fish winter in the mainstem Thompson below Kamloops Lake and in May start into the tributaries for the June spawning.

Thompson fish respond well to the fly, particularly those on floating lines. When big, strong fish that respond to surface-presented flies are combined with a big river, you have the makings for some spectacular sport. Although the great Thompson steelhead attracts anglers from all over the Pacific Northwest, other locations in Canada, the United States and even other parts of the world, the river's very size and the difficulties of reading the water send many home with tales of failure. Those who have learned the

river's secrets and are willing to work hard have memories of a lifetime, especially if they happen to encounter some of the famous Thompson River screamers.

Every Thompson steelhead is a prize but most seasoned pros who have fished the Thompson for a number of years would probably agree that about 25 percent of the fish hooked have that little extra that puts them in a class of their own. These are the heart-stoppers. With the heart-stoppers, one moment you are swimming your fly through a lie; the next you have been stricken by a bolt of lightning. All your fly line and 100 yards-plus (91 metres-plus) of backing have been taken and you are scurrying out of the water to follow the torpedo downstream.

One such heart-stopper of the 1991 season is still vivid in my mind. Fellow Totem Flyfisher club member Bob Taylor and I had spent close to two weeks on the river under trying conditions. The day we arrived, the temperature plummeted and during our stay temperatures as high as 32°F (0°C) were the exception; 5°F (-15°C) during the night was not uncommon. The cold weather was combined with strong winds and few fish. The 1991 run to the Thompson was probably the worst on record and our quarry were especially hard to find. Under such adverse circumstances, no noteworthy fish is soon forgotten. On the last day of our trip, we planned to go home after the morning's fishing. In the last pool before heading home, while Taylor took it easy, I went up to one of my favorite spots for a final go. It wasn't long before my 2/0 Black General Practitioner was taken by a strong but not exceptional steelhead. We parted company after about five minutes. I didn't expect any more fish. This was my second hookup and two fish in a morning is not bad for the Thompson and was exceptional on that trip, when we had worked extremely hard under adverse conditions for few fish.

I waded back in, content just to wile away the last bit of time before heading home. But it wasn't to be that kind of morning. The

Black General Practitioner fly landed on the water and almost immediately I saw a boil from a fish moving to the fly. But no connection was made. The next time the fly came over, the heart-stopper had it. The steelhead struck the fly with the strength of the railway locomotives that travel both banks of the river and soon reached fast water just beyond where the fish had been lying. The reel sang and sang until the fish leapt out of the water, well over 100 yards (91 metres) downstream. The spectacular fight continued until, fifteen minutes later, after several runs and jumps, I slid a 32-inch (81-centimetre) female onto the beach. I didn't have to fish anymore. I was content, though a bit shaken; those heart-stoppers really set loose the adrenalin, I mused, as I wandered back to the camper. What a way to end a Thompson River season!

I have spent twenty-five memorable seasons in pursuit of Thompson River steelhead and through those many years, the river has passed on a few of its secrets. No matter how many secrets you learn from this book, however, your catch at the end of the day will be determined by hard work, your skills and knowledge and how you put them to use. Many seasons—some good and some bad— have slipped away since that first one in 1969. All are cherished but the ones I cherish most are the seasons after I switched to fly fishing in 1979.

The River and the Steelhead Season

SIMON FRASER, THE FAMOUS NORTHWEST COMPANY explorer, named the Thompson River after company topographer and explorer David Thompson in 1808. While Fraser was following the river bearing his name to its mouth, Thompson was only a few hundred miles away exploring the upper waters of the Columbia River, which he mapped to the Pacific. Although Thompson walked and canoed 55,000 miles (88,500 kilometres) from the Atlantic to the Pacific, mapping the country, he never set sight on the river bearing his name.

With its 21,000-square-mile (54,500-square-kilometre) drainage basin, the Thompson River is a major tributary of the mighty Fraser River, which empties into the sea at Vancouver, British Columbia. The Thompson River is home to many salmonids: Chinooks, coho, pinks, sockeye, resident rainbow trout and the rainbow's seagoing brethren, the steelhead. The most famous of the Thompson River's salmon runs is the Adams River sockeye run. On a cycle year, the seven-mile-long (11-kilometre-

Wind-carved hoodoos frequently mark the steep, sloped river valley walls of the Thompson.

Sockeye salmon: On a cycle year it is worth visiting the Haig-Brown Conservation Area on the Adams River to view this sample of Nature's abundance.

long) Adams River can have upwards of three million sockeye spawning in its short, seven-mile length. It is a sight to behold and in mid-October, it is worth a day's side trip from steelheading to view this sample of nature's abundance. Although some sockeye appear every year, the peak cycle year occurs every fourth year—in 1990, 1994, 1998 and so on.

The Thompson is a big river and can appear ominous to those newcomers journeying to fish it. The river's flow can vary from a high of around 100,000 cubic feet per second (3000 cubic metres per second) with a river-gauge reading of 7 metres (23 feet) at the peak of the freshet in late spring, to a flow of less than 5,000 cubic feet per second (150 cubic metres per second) with a river-gauge reading of less than 1 metre (3 feet), during the low flows of late autumn and winter. The maximum flow from the spring runoff usually occurs in June and then the river's flow drops, often continually, until February or March. It is the lower flows of late September through the regulated end of the fishing season on December 31 that are of interest to steelhead fly fishermen.

About 160 miles (257 kilometres) up the Fraser from Vancouver, the Thompson joins the Fraser at Lytton. Twenty-three miles (37 kilometres) up the Thompson from Lytton is the old Cariboo Wagon Road town of Spences Bridge. This area, in and around the town and upstream and downstream, has the better fly fishing runs. For visiting fishermen, Spences Bridge, with its motels and auto courts, has ample accommodation. However, it can get crowded during the peak of the season—from the last two weeks of October through November—and visiting anglers planning a trip should make reservations. For the recreation vehicle driver or camper, there are numerous roadside camping areas.

The steelhead migrate through the Fraser in late August, September, October and early November. The run's forerunners—those that manage to escape the commercial nets, bar fishery, native food fishery and poaching—show up around Spences Bridge

in late September or early October, depending on water conditions. I live in Vancouver, not far from the mouth of the Fraser River. It is an 185-mile (300-kilometre) drive to Spences Bridge. My route follows the river's course to the sea but in reverse. I travel up the Fraser Valley to Hope; then up the Fraser Canyon, past Boston Bar and Hell's Gate to Lytton; and from Lytton up the Thompson past Shaw Springs to Spences Bridge. My journey is comparable in distance to that swum by the steelhead. But, mine takes a matter of hours; the fish's, many days.

At times, fishing in late September or early October can be worthwhile but it is dependent on the numbers of fish and the height of the river. If plotted against time on graph paper, the run of fish into a river would have a bell-shaped curve—few fish at the start of the season, many at the peak of the run, then few fish again at the end of the run. If 10 percent of the run showed up at the start of the season, the number of fish there for fly fishermen pushing the season to catch would vary with the size of the run. For example, if it is a good year and there are 4,000 fish then there would be about 400 steelhead scattered throughout many miles of river, with some most likely in good fly fishing water around Spences Bridge. The possibilities of success on an early trip to the Thompson would be promising. If the run were poor and only 1,000 fish survived the treacherous, net-strewn journey, then there would be only 100 fish scattered throughout many miles of river. With only one quarter the fish, the prospects diminish and it is hardly worth rushing the season.

All this is supposition anyway. Because most steelhead can't be observed migrating up the colored Fraser, and with native and commercial interception, it is impossible to know what a run is like until anglers test the waters. In 1992 the steelhead swam through unmolested waters for the first time in over one hundred years. Since there was no interception the run turned out to be a good one, with an estimated three to four thousand fish. In any event, to get an idea of numbers fishermen sample the fishing from mid-September on and when steelhead are caught, word spreads and the season begins.

Fly fishers journey to the Thompson throughout the summer months in search of its resident rainbow trout and a trout fishing trip in late September, with the steelhead gear thrown in to sample the Graveyard or Rock Run, can produce some unexpected rewards. So can a stop on the return from a September trip to the Skeena system. Late September and early October fishing on the Thompson can be a peaceful, pleasant experience. Generally, there are few fishermen and shirtsleeve weather prevails. However, visiting anglers should plan their trips to coincide with the arrival of the bulk of the Thompson River stocks; they arrive in the Spences Bridge area in the later part of October and early November. But good catches can be made anytime up to the end of the season, providing the weather cooperates. It can get very cold in this country.

In 1986 a cold snap came in late October and temperatures plunged well below 32°F (0°C). An accompanying snowstorm closed the Trans-Canada Highway and many fishermen were stranded in frozen-up trailers and campers. During the cold snap, fishing was impossible—lines froze instantly and all one could do was wait for the weather to break. Fortunately, early cold snaps usually don't last and this one didn't. After a few days, the weather did break and the mass exodus began. Luckily for me, I missed the cold snap. I had been fishing the Thompson the weekend before and had good fishing. When I left to go home, the temperature was already 19°F (-7°C). It plunged to -22°F (-30°C). During the cold snap I was sitting at home waiting for the weather to break, so that I could return, knowing that the fish would be there waiting and most of the fishermen gone. As the trapped fishermen left, I returned and had two good days on the river, hooking five fish and landing three. But the weather again turned foul and sent me home. Any time after the beginning of November it can get very cold in the Spences Bridge area but if you watch the weather, late-season trips to the Thompson can be worthwhile.

The Thompson River offers a skilled fly fisherman many challenges: big water, difficult-to-find fish, some horrendous wading and, at times, trying fishing conditions. But the rewards can be worth it because the Thompson River is home to world-class, catch-and-release steelhead that respond well to a properly presented fly through the October to December-end fishing season.

History

$\mathcal{D}$URING THE EARLY EXPLORATION OF CANADA AND Northwestern United States, the waterways were the highways and railroads of the Hudson Bay Company's and the North West Company's fur traders. Disregarding the native's thousands of years familiarity with the river and advice against it, in 1828 on a canoe trip to the Pacific, George Simpson, then governor of the Hudson Bay Company, decided to explore by canoe the Thompson and Fraser Rivers. Peter Newman, in his book *Caesars of the Wilderness* (1987), describes Simpson's trip, observations and conclusions:

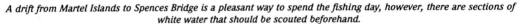

A drift from Martel Islands to Spences Bridge is a pleasant way to spend the fishing day, however, there are sections of white water that should be scouted beforehand.

The Hotel Run waters below the Steelhead Inn require minimal wading.

◆

He thus decided to explore the Fraser River and its great tributary, the Thompson, both of which their discoverer, Simon Fraser, had so eloquently declared to be unnavigable only twenty years previously. Simpson had also been warned by local traders that he would never descend those rocky torrents alive. That, of course, ensured he would make the attempt. After facing the terrors of the Thompson, which he admitted, "made whitened countenances of the boldest among us," he tackled the relentless Fraser with its perpendicular canyons and deadly whitewater shoots . . . even he was forced to concede that passage down that river of hell was certain death and disappointedly ruled it out as a trade route. (p. 313)

Thus, the hoped-for trade route to the Lower Mainland via the Fraser and Thompson Rivers was abandoned in favor of other, less direct routes. But 150 years later, the "terrors of the Thompson" and "river to hell" would be sought out by many thrill-seeking city dwellers for hair-raising, whitewater rafting experiences.

One of the first mentions of large trout or steelhead in British Columbia (and Thompson River steelhead at that), however, appeared in the journal of Alexander Anderson, a fur trader for the Hudson Bay Company. As a result of the unnavigable Thompson and Fraser Rivers Anderson, on the orders of James Douglas, chief fur trader for the Hudson Bay Company, was charged with finding an overland route to the Lower Fraser River for the New Caledonia fur brigade. On his second attempt to find a route, he spent the night on a Thompson River tributary, the Nicola River. His journal entry for May 21, 1847 states:

> Along this stream (known as the Similkameen branch of Thompson's river or more distinctively as Nicholas' [Nicola] river) are some sparse camps of Indians, the inhabitants of which were occupied playing their scoop nets from stages erected near the water's edge. The produce of this fishery is a fine kind of trout, from 10 to 12 lbs weight. Of these we procured a sufficiency for supper.

There is little doubt that Anderson's "fine kind of trout" were Thompson summer-run steelhead migrating into the Nicola and its tributaries on the final leg of their spawning journey.

Although not navigable by boat, in later years, both the Fraser and Thompson River valleys played vital roles, with their rail and road links to Interior and Eastern Canada. The first road through Fraser Canyon and Thompson Valley—the Cariboo Wagon Road—was built after gold was discovered in the Cariboo. Parts of the road traversed the Thompson River and about a mile (1.6 kilometres) below the Nicola River, in 1864, Thomas Spence built his toll bridge. Although only river pilings mark the spot of the original bridge crossing, the community of Spences Bridge is located there today and bears his name.

◆

Big Horn sheep: This ewe with her lamb are typical of the pictures obtainable by wildlife enthusiasts. The sheep come into town and browse in residents' yards during steelhead season.

The river's trees wear their fall colors through much of the steelheading season.

A nicely colored female fish from the Hotel Run.

◆

In the early days of the crown colony and after 1871, when British Columbia became a province of Canada, most people who came were seeking riches, few were interested in sport fishing and mention of fishing the Thompson in those early days is scarce. One of the first references to fishing the Thompson occurred in 1876 when Lord Dufferin, Governor General of Canada, and his wife toured parts of the province. In recollections of their Canadian years, they mention that on a trip along the Cariboo Wagon Road to Kamloops they stopped at Savona and tried trout fishing.

British Columbia, with its many mountain ranges and rugged coastline, was then and still is a difficult place in which to travel. As part of the agreement that British Columbia would join Canada, the province was promised a rail link to the East. In July 1886, the rail link to the rest of Canada was complete and the Canadian Pacific Railway's first transcontinental passenger train arrived in Port Moody, an eastern suburb of Vancouver. The building of the railway through the Thompson River Valley brought the astute observer, writer and angler Dr. T. W. Lambert from England to the banks of the Thompson River. Lambert came to British Columbia in the 1880s as the surgeon attached to the Western Division of the Canadian Pacific Railway Company. He spent twelve years in the interior of the province and fished many of its innumerable lakes and streams. Lambert's book, *Fishing in British Columbia*, published in 1907 is a jewel of information and is the first book devoted almost entirely to the province's sport fishing opportunities. Lambert wrote his book "to give some idea of the habits and peculiarities of the rainbow and the sport which it affords in its native haunts." The book contains a wealth of information on trout fishing in the Thompson River and Kamloops areas, on the "silver-trout" and "steel-heads" of the Thompson, on steelhead in the Fraser and other Lower Mainland and Vancouver Island streams and on salmon fishing at Campbell River and elsewhere.

The Thompson River trout fishing impressed Lambert and his description of the fish and the river is one of the reasons that many anglers travel considerable distances to challenge the river and its fish. He wrote:

On the whole there is probably no fishing river in British Columbia to beat this one for the size and quality of the fish, though it does not afford the large bags that can be obtained on the Kootenay. It is a very sporting river, owing to the strength of the current, for a big fish is hard to hold if it once gets out into the main current, away from the side eddies. Mainly owing to this is the fact that there seems to be no record of fish over about 4lb. . . .

The average fish is from 1/2lb. to 4lb., but much larger fish are in the deep pools. I once was shown at Spence's Bridge [sic] three supposed salmon in the winter which had been speared and sold by the Indians for two shillings apiece. I noticed their perfect condition and bright red side stripe and, on examining them more carefully, pointed out to an experienced fisherman who was present and to the proprietor of the hotel and others, that these fish were large rainbow trout. The largest weighed 15lb., the two others 12lb. apiece. This incident happened at Spence's Bridge, on the Lower Thompson. On another occasion of a visit there, the bar-tender of the hotel, who happened to be a young Englishman, told me that the angling editor of an American sporting paper had stayed off there and proposed to try with spoon and minnow for large rainbow trout, which he had heard could be got. The next day they went to where the Nicola River, a large stream, flows into the Thompson about half

14

a mile from the hotel. The angling editor was provided with strong spinning gear and rod and much to the bartender's surprise, very soon got into a fish of most surprising strength and dimensions, for they saw him several times and estimated him at the unbelievable weight of over 30lb. The fish took them rapidly down to some impassable rocks and went away with everything but the rod. (pp. 14-16)

This last paragraph contains the first written record of a steelhead played and lost on this magnificent river. From the 1890s to the late 1940s, it was believed that steelhead were not strong enough to swim the fast-flowing, turbulent water of the Fraser Canyon. Our angling doctor reported what had been determined by the fisheries scientists of the day: Above Hell's Gate the fish were rainbow trout; below they were steelhead. But Lambert, an astute observer and a knowledgeable, experienced fisherman questions this hypothesis:

It is hard to say how far the steel-head may run up the Fraser—probably at least as far as the Coquehalla [sic] at Hope, for up to this point there is nothing in the strength of the current to prevent it; but above, in the Fraser Canyon, the tremendous difficulties of the ascent may well stop its further progress. The steel-head has not developed the powerful tail and anal fin of the Pacific salmon, which must be a great aid to it in passing through such strong water for such immense distances. It may well be that the smaller tail of the steel-head renders it unfit for the effort. Otherwise, there would be no reason why it should not travel up the rivers as far as the salmon, just as the sea-trout does in European rivers. This is apparently not the case. The Fraser Canyon appears to be impassable to them and they are only found in the lower tributaries of the Fraser and shorter coastal rivers. (pp. 68-69)

After the idea that steelhead weren't strong enough to swim the Fraser was put down in writing, the myth that they couldn't pass Hell's Gate lasted for about fifty years. When Lambert's book was written, however, steelhead were being caught off the mouth of the Nicola River. The time of year is October and the fish described in Lambert's passage are undoubtedly steelhead:

A chipmunk was a frequent visitor to our camping spot.

Jean and Jerry Wintle: Thompson River regulars for well over 30 years.

Mr. Inskip has within the last year or two written some letters to the Field describing the capture of a number of silver fish up to 10lb. weight near Spence's Bridge, at the mouth of the Nicola River, where it joins the Thompson. He believes these fish to be salmon and it is possible that his view may be correct. But it is also possible that they may be silver trout or steelhead trout; the evidence is not yet complete. No salmon have ever been taken in this way with spoon or minnow above this point, in spite of the number of years that fishing has been carried on in these waters. The Indians never catch salmon by trolling with the spoon, though they troll persistently for trout, the line being fastened to the paddle of their canoe.

Mr. Inskip states that these fish never take the fly and he has only caught them in October. There is, of course, no doubt of the truth of his statement and a possible explanation might be that the steelheads run up as far as this point and go up to the Nicola River. It has never been thought that the steelhead runs as far as Kamloops Lake and I have never heard of anyone who claimed to have caught one; it is, however, quite within the bounds of possibility that some of these fish may come up with the salmon. The problem can be easily solved by counting the rays in the anal fin; in the true trout these rays only amount to about nine, in the salmon there are fourteen to sixteen well-developed rays. (pp. 42-43)

Dr. Lambert's book is 136 pages long and jam-packed with information on the Thompson River. It is worth reading for those who are interested in the early history of freshwater sport fishing in the province. Sport fishing on the Thompson developed slowly. Shortly after Lambert returned to England and his book came out, the fit and able of British Columbia, the rest of Canada and Britain were fighting World War I. After the war the depression years produced very hard times and in 1939 the beginning of World War II took the able-bodied away again. During this period, for the average working sport fisherman, money to travel and fish was scarce. British sportsmen did not come to British Columbia as frequently as they had in the past. Rail travel was expensive and if you wanted to travel past the Coast Mountain Range into the interior of the province, you did so by train or if you were wealthy enough, by automobile. Driving through the Fraser Canyon was a hazardous time-consuming journey particularly during winter. In October, just when the steelhead arrived in good numbers the river's closed, trout-season started, not to end until spring. Further, the Thompson River was in two management districts, each with different regulations governing the fishing. The combination of all these factors prevented the discovery of the magnificent steelhead fishing in the Thompson River.

After World War II the situation changed but books published before and during the war perpetuated the theory that steelhead did not venture past Hell's Gate on the Fraser. In 1932 J. R. Dymond, notable Canadian fishery scientist of the day, wrote in his book *The Trout and Other Game Fishes of British Columbia* about steelhead trout: It is not known how far steelheads ascend from the sea in the Fraser river, but it is probable that few, if any, penetrate beyond Hell's Gate . . . (p. 13)

The Sportsmen's Guide to British Columbia (1941) reiterates Dymond's statement. But in an article in the *Vancouver Sun* on January 27, 1948, outdoor editor, Lee Straight, reported:

> Two local steelheaders, Hec Field and Curly McKinnon, hit a jackpot of monster steelhead on a four-day trip to the Thompson River last weekend.
>
> On a trip through the canyon early in the week, Field was forced by a snowstorm to hole up at Keray Leachty's Big Horn Court. He was advised to throw a line at the Thompson and when he dunked a big dew worm, things happened fast.
>
> "They're the biggest steelhead I've ever seen," said Field, who's well known as an accomplished steelheader on local rivers.
>
> "I'll bet some of the fish that broke me went 40 pounds," he reported enthusiastically. "It's the best fishing I've ever had and I wired Curly to come up immediately (on the train)."
>
> The two anglers took easy limits of three fish apiece per day, released many and lost more through smashed tackle.
>
> Average weight per catch? Seventeen pounds per fish.

In February, four weeks after that first-ever Thompson steelhead report, Straight made his inaugural trip. In those pre-snow-tire and road clearing winter days, highway driving was difficult, Straight wrote:

Steelhead Plentiful
In Thompson River

Ehor Boyanowsky may have the distinction of landing the largest-to-date Thompson fly-caught steelhead: Estimated to be 27 pounds. Photo Ehor Boyanowsky.

Gravestones overlooking the Graveyard Run. The history of Spences Bridge is marked by those permanently resting here.

◆

Six Hour Drive from Town Brings
Limit Catch in Steelhead Fishing

There's a steelhead mine six hours drive from Vancouver. It's the Thompson River, no less. And steelhead fishing as good as you find anywhere is right by the Trans-Canada Highway.

Thus the rush started: not for the gold of olden days but for Thompson River steelhead. And mine the river they did. Although there were few steelhead fly fishermen in those days, word spread and in the early 1950s some came to challenge this grand sport fish. These next two reports are classic British Columbia angling history; even though they may not be the first fly fishing encounters with Thompson River steelhead, they are the first two documented in writing that I have managed to locate. On November 6, 1952, after spending the previous few seasons fishing the Thompson with spinning gear, the master British Columbian craftsman and fly fisher Tommy Brayshaw was fishing the Thompson's Hotel Run with the fly. Brayshaw's angling diary describes the scene well:

I tried a fly with Floyd below with eggs and Gay a way down. At noon I hooked one on a #2 Light Coquihalla Orange. A most violent fish, bright and about 14 or 15 lbs. I should think. It kept on jumping and worked upstream though my line was in a huge belly downstream. I was nervous lest it go down beyond the piles of the old bridge, but it came on my side. Floyd joined me and Gay came hastening up, having seen the jumping from below. Then the fly came back—no special reason, the fish was quiet at the time and all seemed well under control. I was disappointed, I should have dearly liked to be the first to kill their [Thompson River] steelhead on fly.

Brayshaw didn't get back to the Thompson that year. He did the following year, however, when he teamed up with his fly fisherman friend from Campbell River, the writer Roderick Haig-Brown. The extract from Brayshaw's diary for November 13, 1953, states:

Started at 10 a.m. then went up the Nicola [Highway] to 2nd bridge. A nice looking pool [Grease Hole] alongside the road. Rough going on rocky side of road. I fished the top & Rod [Haig-Brown] the bottom. Not much fishable water at top but the bottom looked better. Went back to S.B. [Spences Bridge] & had lunch & then went to the Y above Acacia Auto Ct. where I had caught a nine pounder [spinning] on Nov. 29/50. I tried on top (X) but the wading was awful and there was little water before the slack water on my side became too wide to work the fly properly. Went down to Rod who had started opposite the end of the Y. He signaled he had hooked & lost one, which later he told me was a big fish and had it on some few minutes when the nylon broke at the fly under no pressure, blamed the loss on having untied his knot & put a new fly on without cutting the end of the nylon off; that was about 3 p.m.

Brayshaw's Sketch of Y Pool and Lie
(The steelhead lie is a high-water one: Brayshaw noted the river was 2-3 feet higher than the previous season.)

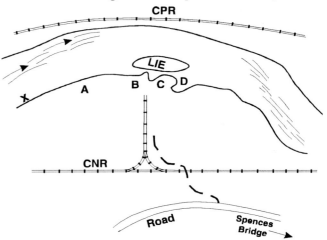

Coming down I started at A & at B using a 1/0 Light Coquihalla Orange. I had a small pull close in. Next cast he came again & pulled tight but I still missed it so changed to a size 2, Mustad 5X strong, Dark C.O. [Coquihalla Orange]. Rod had now come behind at A. At C, I hooked one well & off it went jumping 3 or 4 times, I got out of the water on to the beach when the fly came away

Continued down to D, rising two more but couldn't connect & then came out changed to size 2 (5X str.) Light C.O. [Coquihalla Orange] variant (using light mallard overwing instead of polar bear) and started in behind Rod at B. Geo. Rannie arrived & put in at A with a fluorescent homemade spinner.

I'd got nearly to D and it was now nearly 4:30 [p.m.] and getting pretty dark when I got into a fish. Went off down jumping, I got out of water & Roddy joined me. George got out of water to help but reeling in he struck one. It was very dark and my fish got a long way down-

The Rock Pile and Martel Islands are good fly fishing spots. Anglers appear as mere dots in the large piece of water.

In 1892, Archie Clemes built the second Spences Bridge Hotel up the bank from the original 1862 location. It is one of British Columbia's oldest hotels; in 1991, it was renovated and renamed The Steelhead Inn.

stream but Roddy waded down on a bar and finally got his fingers in its gills a rather dark male 12 1/2 lbs.— took about 15 minutes [to land]. As we came back we found George had got his, also a dark cock of 16 1/4 lbs. We cleaned them & found the gonads in mine very undeveloped (Rod estimated about 25%). George's were very much larger and would have spawned much earlier.

Great excitement in the Rannie household as my fish was thought to be the first fly caught steelhead from the Thompson . . .

I don't believe that you could have found a more suitable pair of fishermen to christen Thompson River steelhead with the fly than Tommy Brayshaw and Roderick Haig-Brown. A classic story indeed. From the 1950s through the early 1980s, fly fishing was not the choice of Thompson River steelheaders. In the mid-eighties, however, fly fishing for steelhead blossomed in the Pacific Northwest and now, on any given day during the season, you will find just as many fly fishers searching the runs for prized Thompson River steelhead as you will find other gear-type fishermen. Fly fishermen account for about 10 percent of the catch.

The Fish

*F*OR HUNDREDS OF YEARS HUMANS HAVE SHOWN A fascination for fish and, in particular, game fish in rivers. One such fish, the steelhead, is a mysterious fish that appears from the sea strong, sleek and silver to ascend our rivers at varying times

A typical 35-inch female.

The scenic Adams River: A most prolific salmon producer.

of the year on its spawning run. It is also a fish of great beauty and like many other objects of beauty that attract human beings, even if very briefly, it is something to be possessed. Furthermore, to the fly fisherman, the steelhead is a challenging fish to catch. Because of these attributes—mystery, strength, beauty, being a challenge to catch—the steelhead is a highly regarded game fish. Some who have a lasting love affair with the steelhead believe it is the equal to what many consider the king of game fish—the Atlantic salmon. The Thompson River has a unique run of hard-fighting, better-than-average, large-sized, summer-run steelhead. The bulk of the Thompson stocks consists of five-year-olds, averaging 15 pounds (7 kilograms) but fish of over 30 pounds (14 kilograms) have been taken. Some fish stories report that 40-pounders (18 kilograms) have been lost. The Thompson fish is unique not just because of its size but because many of the fish tend to be "screamers" or "heart-stoppers." They take the fly violently and before you know it, there is a 15-pound (7-kilogram) steelhead cartwheeling around the river with 100 yards (91 metres) of line out. What a thrill!

History of Names

This fish that anglers call steelhead has had many names. The first was one native tribe's name of *cha-cha-lool.* Long considered a trout related to the Atlantic salmon and brown trout of Europe, it was first classified in 1792 in Asia by J. J. Walbaum and given the scientific name of *Salmo mykiss.* Thought to be an unclassified species of fish, in 1836, after examining a Columbia River specimen, Sir John Richardson named the steelhead *Salmo gairdneri.*

The sample was sent to him by a Dr. Gairdner, an employee of the Hudson Bay Company who was stationed in Fort Vancouver in what is now the state of Washington.

After British Columbia became a British crown colony, John Keast Lord, the naturalist with the commission that was to survey the boundary from the coast to the eastern slope of the Rocky Mountains spent three years, from 1860 to 1863, in British Columbia and was the first to record Richardson's *Salmo gairdneri* there, among many other birds, fish and animals. In Volume 1 of Lord's scarce two-volume book *The Naturalist in British Columbia* (1866) he writes:

> The next salmon [trout] in importance, as affording food to the Indians, is called by them at the Kettle Falls *cha-cha-lool,* and arrives with the Quinnat [Chinook]. This is unquestionably a fully matured fish and a distinct species, answering in many particulars to the *Salmo gairdneri* of Sir J. Richardson it will be as well to retain that name. It may be readily distinguished from the Quinnat by its rounded blunt-looking nose, shorter and much thicker head, straighter back and more slender figure the tail not nearly as much forked. The entire colour of the back is much lighter and thickly freckled, as are the fins and tail, with oval black spots. The average weight of the *cha-cha-lool* is from 8 to 11 lbs.. This salmon [trout] is common in the Fraser, Chilukweyuk [Chilliwack] and Sumass [Sumas] rivers and in every stream along the mainland and island coasts up which salmon ascend. (pp. 52-53)

◆

The Thompson River Valley with a dusting of snow.

Salmo gairdneri was known by several common names, most frequently the steelhead. Over the years there has been much speculation about where the name steelhead originated, Trey Combs in his book *The Steelhead Trout* (1971) writes: "The origin of the name "steelhead" is not clear. The extremely hard bones in the skull and coloration of this trout when it is a fresh-run fish have been both suggested as origins of the name. (p. 66)"

Published in 1891, *Bear-Hunting in the White Mountains of Alaska and British Columbia Revisited*, H. W. Seton-Karr describes the two trouts available in British Columbia and he says, "The steel-head attains from twenty to twenty-five pounds. (p.17)" Ten years before Seton-Karr's early, if not first, British Columbian reference to steelhead the word was attested in the *United States National Museum, Volume IV, 1881* (1882) by David Starr Jordan and Charles Gilbert, under *Salmo gairdneri* and mistakenly with the trout later to be called the cutthroat but at that time classified as *Salmo purpuratus,* we find the first written attestation for the word steelhead:

54. *Salmo gairdneri* Richardson.—Steel-head; Hard-head; Black Salmon. (*Salmo Truncatus* Suckley)

Found in the mouths of the large rivers from the Columbia northward and occasionally in the Sacramento. It appears with the salmon and it is usually thought to be migratory, but is probably not so or migratory to a small degree. It spawns later than the salmon. . . . In other rivers than the Columbia and at other seasons it is esteemed an excellent food-fish. Its length is about that of an ordinary Quinnat salmon; the body is less deep and the tail heavier. The usual weight is from 14 to 18 pounds . . . and the bones are firm and stiff. (p. 38)

◆

Cal Woods, long-time Steelhead Society of B. C. secretary and champion of the Thompson and its steelhead. Steelhead Society of B.C. photo.

Dave Winters: He introduced the thinly dressed Doc Spratley fly to the Thompson.

◆

The unusual large size—14 to 18 pounds (6 to 8 kilograms)—described by Jordan and Gilbert is partially explained by the fact that the smaller 8 to 10-pound (3.6 to 4.5-kilogram) steelhead were classified as another fish, *Salmo purpuratus* and the half-pounders of California as still another, *Salmo irideus*, the rainbow trout. However, the larger summer-runs of the Columbia were known locally as steelhead. About *Salmo purpuratus* and the local name of the Columbia River's larger summer-runs, Jordan and Gilbert have this to say:

55. *Salmo purpuratus* Pallas.—Oregon Brook Trout; Salmon Trout; Lake Trout. (*Salmo clarki* Rich)

Very abundant in all waters north of Mount Shasta and through the Great Basin and Rocky Mountain region. . . . Found in abundance in salt water in Puget Sound and about the mouth of the Columbia. It is usually seen of but 2 to 8 or 10 pounds in weight, but occasional specimens weighing as much as 25 pounds are taken in the Columbia in summer

These latter are known usually as steel-heads, although the common steelhead is *S. gairdneri*; the young as brook-trout [cutthroat] and the partly grown as salmon-trout. (p. 39)

Later, in Bulletin Number 16 of the United States National Museum in the *Synopsis of the Fishes of North America* (1882), David Starr Jordan and Charles H. Gilbert gave a much better description for this trout which they described as having "bones much firmer than in the *Oncorhynchi* and abounding in the mouths of the rivers." They also deleted the common name black salmon and included the common name salmon-trout, for those average sized 8 to 10 pound (3.6 to 4.5 kilogram) steelhead. In the 1880s, the steelhead was referred to in colloquial regional terms; the scientific name of the time, *Salmo gairdneri* (now *Oncorhynchus mykiss*), or mistakenly *Salmo purpuratus*, would not then, as it does not today, receive common usage among laymen. In the early 1880s the population of the Northwest was small, with few sport fishermen; what fishing took place was primarily for food and the name "steel-head" was undoubtedly coined by commercial fishermen catching those large trout that Jordan and Gilbert describe as "abounding in the mouths of the rivers." From their research, Jordan and Gilbert considered the steelhead to be a fish that was more common in the northern part of their coastal study area, with the Fraser River being the northern extremity. Perhaps it was the commercial fishermen, who intercepted Thompson River summer-runs, who coined the word steelhead. What other Pacific Northwest stock would better fit the words that Jordan and Gilbert used to describe the size of steelhead: "The usual weight is from 14 to 18 pounds." Whoever they were, these fishermen must have commented that the fish had hard heads or heads of steel and then later just referred to these fish as "steelhead."

The original hyphenated use of "steel-head and hard-head" that Jordan and Gilbert give does provide some credence to the "heads-of-steel" theory, as does their reference in their 1882 publication, cited above, to "bones much firmer than in *Oncorhynchi*." In fact in Jordan and Gilbert's 1881 publication, they state that "the 'common-names' here given are, in all cases, those heard by the writers among the fishermen on different parts of the coast. No doubt the common usage of "steel-head" or "hardhead" dates earlier than this 1881 written attestation. There was a thriving salmon-canning industry along the west coast of the United States and British Columbia after the establishment of the first canneries at the mouth of the Sacramento River in 1864 and at the mouth of the Columbia River two years later. Fishermen during that time—1864 to 1881—would have then coined the common names to describe the fishes they caught. Earlier Jordan papers used only scientific nomenclature, however.

Thompson steelhead were not considered to be sea-run trout because it was believed that the waters of the Fraser Canyon, and specifically those of Hell's Gate, were too swift for steelhead to ascend. This hypothesis most likely stems from the fact that Jordan and other scientists of the time did not consider the large trout "abounding in the mouths of the rivers" to be a migratory fish. Thus, in 1892 Jordan classified the trout of the Fraser watershed above Hell's Gate as a new variety of trout, *Salmo kamloops*. The notion that the steelhead were found only at the mouths of rivers influenced the writings of Dr. T. W. Lambert and he recorded this idea in *Fishing in British Columbia* (1907). Nevertheless, as an experienced angler, Lambert appeared to question the validity of this assumption.

In the early 1900s, confusion about fish and their colloquial

◆

A large 26-pound steelhead taken by one of the major proponents of the waked-fly presentation, Ehor Boyanowsky. Photo Ehor Boyanowsky.

The Great Landslide of August 13, 1905 sign marks the highway pullout for the Graveyard Run.

◆

names was commonplace throughout the Pacific Northwest. In D. S. Jordan's and B. W. Evermann's 1902 book *American Food & Game Fishes*, no less than two dozen varieties of trout are listed in the cutthroat, rainbow and steelhead series of western trouts. This confusion is increased when the five species of Pacific salmon, with their many colloquial names, are thrown in. It is no wonder that confusion exists to this day.

Early fishing regulations also abetted the bafflement. British Columbia's fishing regulations classified steelhead as trout until 1940 and there was no distinction between sea-run and resident trout. The province also had a specified trout-fishing season. During the closed trout season, coastal streams with steelhead runs were open to steelhead fishing; interior streams were not. When Lambert wrote his book, he thought that anglers would have a better chance at catching those big silvery fish that started to show off the mouth of the Nicola River in mid-October if the closed season which started on October 16 were extended a month. Lambert did think that these fish might be steelhead.

In the early days of sport fishing in the province there were no limits on the number of fish that could be caught but later a limit of fifteen trout a day was established. In 1940, a steelhead was defined as a trout that weighed more than 5 pounds (2.2 kilograms) and the limit changed to fifteen trout a day and three steelhead. The large fish that Hec Field and Curly McKinnon declared were steelhead in 1948 may have been steelhead according to the definition at that time. In 1958, the regulations were revised again when a steelhead was defined as an anadromous (seagoing) rainbow trout that was more than 18 inches (46 centimetres) long. The minimum length of a steelhead was revised to 20 inches (51 centimetres) in 1960.

With all these different names and regulations, it is no wonder that there was constant confusion about whether the steelhead

was a trout or salmon. To confuse things even more, in 1988 after over 150 years of documentation on *Salmo gairdneri* Richardson, the *American Fisheries Society's* taxonomists decided that the "*Salmo*" trouts of the Northern Pacific drainages are more closely related to the Pacific salmons (*Oncorhynchus*) than to Atlantic salmon and brown trout and that the "Kamchatkan" trout *S. mykiss* of Asia predates Richardson's *S. gairdneri*. Thus, this trout is now classified as a salmon—*Oncorhynchus mykiss*. This change, however, will not prevent fishers from referring to their favorite game fish as steelhead. Steelhead is the name that stirs the blood and imagination of fishermen.

The Thompson's Summer-Run Steelhead

Steelhead stocks are specific to certain rivers and stocks enter those rivers when water conditions provide ready access to the habitat where the fish were hatched. In some rivers these conditions occur in winter and spring and coincide with the fishes sexual maturity and in other rivers they occur in summer and fall, months ahead of sexual maturity. Thus, steelhead are divided into two classes—winter-run and summer-run. In the Thompson River optimum water conditions occur in the late summer and fall months, thus, the Thompson River steelhead is a summer-run fish.

Fishermen often say that they catch only winter fish in the Thompson. Since they fish there in the winter months they assume that the fish they catch must be winter-run steelhead. But it is the time of entry into fresh water and not when the angler catches the fish in the river, that determines whether a fish is a summer- or winter-run and the Thompson fish enter fresh water—the Lower Fraser—in late August and in September and October.

To get to the Thompson, steelhead stocks must conquer the following obstacles: distance, high-velocity, turbulent water in sections of the Fraser Canyon and in particular Hell's Gate and some high-velocity, turbulent water in the Thompson between Lytton and Gold Pan. Hell's Gate is an obstacle primarily because it is too swift and turbulent for too great a distance. As a result of the lower flows, less turbulent water and warmer water temperatures the steelhead migrate through the Fraser Canyon in September, October and November. When they get into the Thompson they winter there and, after remaining in the mainstem river for up to eight months, head into tributary streams in late spring to spawn.

Another factor that determines the timing of Thompson and other rivers' summer runs is sexual maturity. Bob Hooton, a biologist with the provincial Fish and Wildlife Branch, who refers to interior summer-run steelhead as marathoners, explains the role of sexual maturity in the summer runs of rivers like the Thompson, the Skeena above Terrace and other streams that originate in the Interior:

> Interior summer runs common to the Columbia, Fraser, Skeena, Nass, Stikine and Taku drainages originate in streams inside the coast mountain ranges. These fish tend to be later arrivals (August through October). Again, they enter fresh water on relatively high but declining temperature regimes and stream flows. These features in combination with the high reserves of stored fat and sustained swimming ability . . . are common to all stocks. I believe the evolution of the long run interior summer steelhead stocks in general is related to the stored energy reserves of the fish themselves and the

Angler fishing the Y Pool corner.

Gary Baker with a 35-inch male from the Rock Run.

◆

Jerry Wintle waits his turn while partner, Dave Winters, fishes the Big Horn Pool. These two ardent fishers popularized the floating-line technique on the Thompson in the early 1970s.

time and distance which must be traveled to arrive at preferred spawning locations.

A winter steelhead encumbered with a body cavity full of sex products and with little stored fat would be a very poor candidate to reach Babine Lake against spring break-up flow conditions.

Brent Lister, a biologist and fellow Totem Flyfisher, writes:

As swimming ability in salmonids declines with advancing sexual maturity and with low water temperatures, summer-run fish would have an advantage in surmounting obstacles to migration. . . . As you observe, the summer-fall migration timing of Thompson River steelhead and the interior Skeena River stocks as well, likely reflects the advantages of migration at higher water temperatures and less advanced sexual maturity.

In addition, the low water temperatures found through the November to April winter holding period slow the fishes' metabolism, helping to conserve energy and convert the store of body fat into roe or milt.

Summer-run fish, particularly those of the interior marathon category, color up early and some fishermen think that because a fish is colored it is close to spawning. This is not true. A winter-run fish that is colored is probably close to spawning but a colored summer-run fish often has many months to go before it spawns. The Thompson River fish, males in particular, are an excellent example of fish that are colored in their prime. Most Thompson males are colored when they arrive in the Thompson proper. Females do not color up as much or as quickly as males.

◆

Murray Creek Waterfall: There is some fly water above and below here.

The Freshwater and Saltwater Life of Thompson Steelhead

B.C. rivers are not rich in food life. In fact, most are quite barren. Some of the interior streams, however, including the Thompson, produce more food but since the growing season is short, most fish take two or three years before they become silvercoated smolts and journey to sea.

In their sea lives, some steelhead feed for only a few months and some feed for a year. Most Thompson River steelhead, however, spend two to three years feeding at sea before they return to the river to spawn. Biologists use a system of age designation that consists of two numbers separated by a decimal—for example, 3.2+. The first number indicates the number of winters the fish has spent in fresh water (3), the number after the decimal indicates the number of winters the fish has spent at sea (2) and the plus (+) indicates a partial year of sea feeding with a return to fresh water before the third winter. Thus, in this example, the fish would be a six-year-old when it spawns the following spring. The run in any particular year consists of fish with freshwater and saltwater lives of varying lengths. In the Thompson, approximately 85 percent of the steelhead spend two winters in fresh water and the remaining spend three winters in fresh water. About 90 percent spend two winters in salt water, 3 percent or so spend one winter and 3 percent or so spend three winters in salt water. About 3 percent survived previous spawning, returned to the sea and returned to spawn again. In summary, the majority of Thompson fish spend two winters in fresh water before smoltification takes place, two plus winters of sea feeding and another seven to nine months of upstream migration and holding in fresh water and they are five-year-olds when they spawn.

Return to the River

Some steelhead fishermen think that when a steelhead returns on its spawning run it eats its way up the river. This is far from the truth. The steelhead is a primitive animal with a pea-sized brain. Singleness of purpose is a characteristic of primitive beings. After a steelhead has hatched, pursuit of food is foremost in order for it to survive. This search leads it to the sea, where it grows large. There comes a time, however, in all primitive beings' lives when the hunt for food is abandoned. That is when it approaches maturity and reproduction of the species becomes paramount. Nature cannot have the steelhead flitting off here and there looking for food on its spawning run, the task of reproduction is far too important to leave to chance.

Nature must ensure that the reproduction of the species is not overshadowed by the desire to feed. The returning fish must have enough reserves of stored body fat for the return journey and, in some cases, for prolonged stays in fresh water as well as for the spawning act and, for some fish, the return to the sea as kelts. Thompson steelhead must return to the river with enough fat reserves to sustain them through many months of river residence. Furthermore, they must have enough additional body fat or maturing eggs or milt during their fall to spring wait.

Many fishermen who come to the sport and particularly trout fishermen, find it difficult to grasp the concept that there is a difference between a resident river trout, whose survival depends on getting enough food to eat and a steelhead, whose only purpose for returning to the river is to reproduce the species.

When small bits of organic and inorganic items are found in a steelhead's stomach, they assume that the fish has gone out and hunted these items and is feeding. But a single salmon egg, a couple of caddis larvae or a few mayfly nymphs would provide a tiny fraction of the energy required to keep a large fish alive.

Steelhead fishermen are aware that if they present their lure—bait, fly, spoon and so on—properly, the fish will often take it. Generally, the fish will not move great distances to get the lure. More often than not for a bait fisherman, the fish will steal some of the bait during the drift and these small bits of food items are the things that are found in the stomachs of the fish we catch. There is a difference between a trout searching for food and a steelhead that takes something because it happens to appear before it. For the steelhead, what food is taken by the adult is in very meager amounts and at best the steelhead can be considered to be but an opportunistic feeder.

Taking Times

When the steelhead makes its return to the river, it may hold off at the mouth of the river until water conditions suit migration. On large rivers like the Fraser, Skeena and Columbia, there is plenty of flow, even at low levels and upstream migrations are not deterred by lack of water. On some of the coastal spate rivers, the run is drawn in by an increase in flow and, on many rivers, migration is instigated by the spring runoff.

Fast-running steelhead are poor takers. However, a freshly arrived steelhead moving slowly upriver, stopping here and there to test the current or rest, is an alert fish and can be a grand taker. Providing the angler matches method to water conditions, the fish can be relatively easy to catch. This is the time when inexperienced anglers often have good sport and experienced anglers better. After the run has arrived, the fishing can vary from excellent to poor. On any given day, however, there are usually some fish that will come on the "take." To be successful, you must be there at the right time and preferably the fish undisturbed. For weekend fishers because the fish have not been fished for as much through the week, Saturday can often be much better than Sunday. But there are times during the run when water conditions change and existing fish that have been difficult to catch become catchable again.

I have fished the Thompson River for twenty-five years and in over half of those years, I religiously went every weekend through October and November and into December. Sometimes the fishing was good; often it was poor. Over the years and through the seasons, however, I noticed that the river height varied considerably and that at different levels and water temperatures I would catch fish in certain pools. In 1979, I started taking river-gauge readings and over subsequent seasons correlated these readings to holding spots in the runs. This information is tabulated in the "Runs and Pools" section of the book.

I also noticed that the river height not only varied from year to year but also during a particular season. It was not the steadily dropping river that made fishing poor; rather, it was the seasonal increases that resulted from rains in a very large catchment area. Even though it would not rain at Spences Bridge—desert country gets little annual rainfall—it would rain on much of the watershed and the river would come up considerably. An increase of 0.5 metre (1.6 feet) on a good river-fishing height of 1.5 metre (4.9 feet) would increase the volume of water in the river by 40 percent. And a good rise in water will give poor fishing. If the river came up after the run arrived at Spences Bridge, the only fish around to be caught were the ones that were migrating through at the new height. The fish that had already arrived made slight adjustments in their resting spots if necessary and, if these spots had been within casting range before the rise, those fish were now far out of reach. Rumors would circulate that the fish had disappeared and you would hear that the whole run had migrated up the Nicola or other tributaries and fishers would head for home. When the effects of the storm had run their course, the river would eventually recede to its former level and lower. It is during the drop that I plan my return trips because the fish become catchable again. When this happens, however, fishermen would start talking about the new run that had arrived. In reality, it was just the old run becoming accessible again.

In addition, after the run gets into the Thompson, some fish will find a good hole that suits them and will settle in for long periods. Settled-in fish can be difficult to entice and often those holding spots are out of range of fly presentation. On any given day, however, there is usually some internal local movement, sometimes only within the pool, sometimes into a run a little upstream or downstream and sometimes miles upriver towards the fishes' natal tributary stream. Thompson fish have months to make internal moves toward their natal stream but each time they move some become takers, just like fresh-run fish.

Methods of Presentation

*T*HERE ARE FIVE METHODS OF PRESENTING FLIES TO steelhead: floating-line, skated- or waked-fly, sunk-line, dry fly and upstream sunk-fly presentation. A successful fisherman knows them all and is adept at recognizing conditions that require the fly to be presented a certain way. Only three methods—floating-line, sunk-line and skated or waked-fly—are widely used Thompson River presentations. The other two methods require precise work and although they do work elsewhere, the conditions that are a necessity—knowing fish are in a certain spot, in water that can be fished from below and fish that are within a suitable presentation range, say 30 or so feet (9 or so metres)—are not too often encountered on the Thompson River. Fly fishers are best off concentrating on presentation methods that suit the coverage of larger bodies of water. The two most productive are the floating-line and sunk-line methods.

Floating or Sunk Lines?

Many who have fished the Thompson for years know that steelhead can be taken in some runs with the floating-line presentation throughout the season. But the Thompson has a deteriorating temperature regime and as the water gets colder, steelhead become less inclined to move to the fly. I divide the Thompson's steelhead fishing season into two sections: warm-water, above 45°F (7°C) and cold-water, below 45°F (7°C). Basically, the warm-water season is before November 15, the cold after November 15. Although, the temperature of the Thompson River can vary plus or minus 5°F (2.8°C) on any given day from year to year, the average water temperature I have recorded over the past twelve years for mid-October is 52°F (11°C) and for mid-November, 44°F (6.6°C).

The choice of fly presentation method should complement warm- or cold-water conditions and the depth of water the fish are lying in. The table below summarizes this information.

The Floating-Line Presentation

The floating-line presentation is one of the most pleasant ways to fly fish for steelhead. It is also my favorite, therefore, I will describe it first. This method has been called greased-line, floating-line and dry-line fishing. The correct name for it is floating-line fishing. The purpose is to present a fly close to the surface with a line that floats on the surface.

In the history of fly fishing, this is a relatively new method. Devised in Great Britain in the latter part of the nineteenth century for Atlantic salmon fishing when clear, warm-water conditions exist, this method was popularized in the first half of this century. The floating-line method found its way across the Atlantic and into British Columbia in the 1930s. Roderick Haig-Brown first wrote about it in *The Western Angler* (1939) and the method has had its devotees here since that time.

The floating-line method was popularized on the Thompson River in the early 1970s by notable British Columbian steelhead fly fisherman Jerry Wintle of Vancouver and ardent Washingtonian steelheader Dave Winters. In the late 1950s when Wintle started to fly fish the Thompson, there were few fly fishermen. If you asked any fishermen the best way to catch a steelhead they told you that you had to fish down to them. Jerry did

Floating-Line	•Through October to about November 15 in all depths to about 6 feet (2 metres) maximum. The water temperature is usually in the mid to high 50s (13° - 15°C) at the beginning of October, in the low 50s (10° - 12°C) at the end and about 45°F (7°C) in mid-November. •From mid-November in water that is wadeable to a maximum of 4 feet (1.2 metres) and that is not too streamy. Fish are slow to react in cooler waters and are reluctant to move far for the fly.
Sunk-Line	•At any time if the water is greater than 6 feet (2 metres) deep and/or in locations that you know are good holding spots. •In cooler water temperatures, usually found from mid-November onwards and in water that is greater than 3 feet (1 metre) deep.

Author watching Ron Grantham dress Wintle's version of the Doc Spratley.

◆

that and he caught fish. Later, in 1968, up on the Morice River, a tributary of the mighty Skeena River system, he met Dave Winters and they decided to fish the Thompson together. Using the standard-of-the-day sunk-line presentation for the first couple of years or so, they realized that this method did not suit much of the Thompson's water—there were just too many hang-ups and lost flies. Therefore, they decided to try the floating-line technique, which was already popular on the Morice River. They found that this method was ideal for searching for steelhead and suited the big, slow-moving waters of the Thompson and its often-aggressive steelhead.

When I decided to fly fish the Thompson River, I had heard that the water suited the floating-line technique and that is what I used. On a sunny, windy, October afternoon I started in on the lower part of the Graveyard Run and worked my way downstream to the rock island. There is a slick at the top end of this water and I cast my Doc Spratley out and let it come around when I felt what I thought to be a good trout take the fly. It didn't get hooked. My next cast sent my fly through the same water again; I know a fish grabbed it but all I remember was having my line ripped from the reel and a Thompson River steelhead jumping halfway across the river. Gently, I played the fish and proud I was of the 34-inch (86-centimetre) female that I landed. Early success when you are trying to do something brings confidence and that early Thompson success with the floating line made me a convinced, dedicated floating-line fisherman.

Unlike glacial-fed, summer-run streams like the Dean River, where even under optimum water temperatures it is often necessary to use the sunk-line method to catch steelhead because of colored water conditions, the Thompson River is usually clear. Under clear-water conditions water temperature and depth dictate fly presentation. To be successful day after day, you need to cover considerable water and the floating-line method permits that. Fly fishers must also be receptive to using it when clear- and warm-water conditions prevail. Confidence in method, fly and oneself is vital for success and confidence in the floating-line technique on the Thompson will bring rewards.

The Sunk-Line Presentation

When observed in their river environment most salmonids will be seen close to the bottom. The observation of this phenomenon hundreds of years ago has prompted anglers to fish down to them. Thompson River steelhead are no different from other salmonids; they lie close to the bottom. Because of the immensity of the river, however, you can't see them except when they decide to show themselves and roll. Steelhead sometimes do this, mostly when they are moving upriver. If you see a Thompson fish roll, try to cover it; you may get the fish.

Covering the big water of the Thompson River is difficult with the more easily presented floating-line technique but because of the slow-moving water it is much more difficult with the sunk-line technique. That is what prompted Jerry Wintle and Dave Winters to abandon sinkers and go over to the floater. It is especially difficult if you want to get the fly down quickly and use the faster-sinking fly lines that most steelheaders prefer for sunk-line fishing. Compounding the difficulty of presenting the fly on big waters is the tiny amount of water that can be effectively fly covered with single-handed fly rods. With the reintroduction of the double-handed fly rod in the early 1980s, fly fishermen who learned how to use it properly now had a tool that would permit them to cover 80 to 90 or more feet (24 to 27 or more metres) of water with good line control; single-handed rods permit only 50 to 60 feet (15 to 18 metres) of control.

Accompanying the reintroduction of two-fisted rods in British Columbia was Spey casting and double-tapered fly line. Not only did this casting technique suit the floating-line presentation, it made presentation of the sunk fly easier and gave superior line control. In 1984, after I became adept at Spey casting, I thought that I could present the fly better and fish the sunk fly with more control by looping a section of sinking line onto the end of my double-tapered, floating fly line. The results were startling. Spey casts of 80 feet (24 metres) or better were the norm and on the first day I tried this combination up on the Dean River, six fish took the fly. In the next five days, another 4 1/2 dozen fish took the fly presented this way. This combination of floating line with sink tip looped on soon became popular among many British Columbian double-handed users and it is the method I choose for Thompson River steelhead when I believe the fish are lying too deep or they won't respond to a floating-line presentation.

The sunk-line technique is the tool to use when the river is cold and lethargic fish are lying in water over 3 feet (1 metre) deep. Because of the slow-moving water in many Thompson River runs, however, you have to choose a sink tip that suits the water speed. I often loop on a 10 foot (3 metre) section of #9 High Speed High Density line to fish water that is greater than 3 feet (1 metre) deep when the river is below 45°F (7°C). It works well. I remember a couple of days when I used this technique with rather startling results. I had driven to the Thompson River with a couple of friends one late November morning and with just over two hours of daylight remaining I decided to fish the sunk-line method and I looped on 7 feet (2 metres) of high-speed, high-density sink tip onto the end of my double-tapered 11 floating fly line. After coaching my friend, who was new to fishing the Thompson and giving him first crack at the pool, I, a bolder wader, made the difficult trek out into the 39°F (4°C) water. In the next 2 1/2 hours I beached a fine brace of Thompson River steelhead—one 36 1/2 inch (93 centimetre) male and a 35 inch (89 centimetre) female. Expectations at the start of the day often don't match the results at the end of the day and I was more than happy with two fish in such short time. You wonder as the day ends what tomorrow holds.

The next day proved better than the afternoon before. In the first twelve minutes of fishing I had three takes, losing one fish and landing a 34 inch (86 centimetre) female. After lunch, in the next pool, in forty-five minutes of fishing with the same combination— Black General Practitioner fly and 7 foot (2 metre) sink tip—I landed a brace of 37 inch (94 centimetre) males. What a day—five takes, one fish lost and three landed. Fishing the sunk line can be very profitable on the Thompson River in water conditions that suit the method.

The Skated- or Waked-Fly Presentation

In the past fifteen or so years, the use of the skated- or waked-fly presentation has become increasingly popular. This is the last of the fly fishing methods where the fly is cast out either opposite you or below and brought down and across the current. With both sunk-line and floating-line presentations, the fly is below the surface of the water but with the skated-fly method it is not. The main intent of this presentation is to dibble a fly over the lie.

This is a very old technique, dating back to seventeenth century Britain. Richard Franks, speaking about Scottish Atlantic salmon fly fishing in his book *Northern Memoirs* (1658) says, "Dibble but lightly on the surface and you infallibly raise him." Over the centuries, the waked- or skated-fly presentation has had many names. Dibbling, skimming, skittering, waking, riffling, dry fly fishing and surface-lure are some that come to mind. All, with the exception of dry fly fishing, refer to the method in which the fly is brought across the surface of water, causing a wake.

If not the first, then an early proponent of its use on the Thompson River is transplanted Eastern Canadian Atlantic salmon fisherman Ehor Boyanowsky, who has been using the waked-fly technique since the late 1970s. His largest fish-to-date using this technique was a male that was 42 inches (107 centimetres) long and 22 inches (56 centimetres) in girth—by Sturdy's formula, an impressive 27 pounds (12 kilograms). This method is effective at times on the Thompson and will now and then bring huge fish to the surface.

Because you need optimum light conditions with alert fish in water of suitable depth and temperature, the waked-fly technique is far less consistent than the floating- and sunk-line techniques. The waked-fly presentation can be used wherever the floating-line presentation is recommended (see table at beginning of the section). If you decide to use only this method, however, you have to fish it at those times of day when poorer light conditions exist. On those bright, sun-lit Thompson days, using the waked-fly method exclusively can limit your fishing day and thus, your catch. If used wisely, this is a good way of locating and catching fish. It does get the attention of traveling fish and some large fish at that. Some of the anglers I know will fish the waked fly, but when they get a couple of showy rises they change over to a sparsely dressed fly of the right size fished on the floating line and catch the fish. The waked-fly presentation has become a popular way of fly fishing for steelhead on the Thompson and, under the right light and water conditions, can be effective. It is certainly an exciting way to fish.

All three of these down and across presentations—floating-line, sunk line and waked fly—are useful methods used under proper light and water conditions for covering and searching steelhead waters on the Thompson.

Dry Fly and the Upstream Sunk Fly Presentations

The last two methods—dry fly and upstream sunk fly—suit the single-handed rod, upstream approach to known fish holding spots. Circumstances that permit these methods to be used are not commonly found, nor are they practical, on the Thompson. Rest assured that blind fishing with either the dry fly or upstream sunk fly will produce few results on the Thompson. Combining the right fly pattern with presentation and water and light conditions is critical for consistency, not only on the Thompson but on all steelhead rivers.

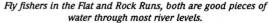

Fly fishers in the Flat and Rock Runs, both are good pieces of water through most river levels.

The majestic and mighty Thompson River.

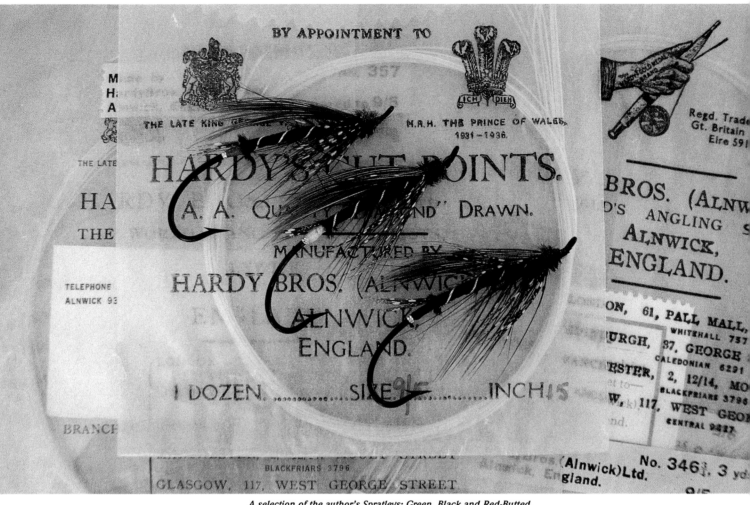

A selection of the author's Spratleys: Green, Black and Red-Butted.

◆

Fly Patterns

I HAVE SAMPLED ABOUT THREE DOZEN BRITISH Columbian steelhead streams and the Thompson, a river that presents many difficulties to steelhead fly fishermen, is no different from most other rivers; it is just a hell of a lot bigger. To achieve consistent results, steelhead fly fishers should take the following factors into consideration when choosing their fur and feather enticements:

•Light conditions—whether it is sunny, cloudy or the water is shaded

•Water conditions—temperature, clearness, velocity and surface turbulence

•Time of day—early morning, mid-day, evening

•State of the fish—fresh-run or present in the river for some time

When fishing conditions deteriorate—and they do daily—the skillful, knowledgeable fly fisher shines over those average-skilled ones. By marrying fly fishing method to conditions and fly selection, a competent fly fisherman can often catch fish even under the most trying conditions. The most trying conditions that I can think of are mid-afternoon on a glassy run, baked in sunshine—typical Thompson River mid-day fishing conditions.

To avoid wasting time trying different types of flies, concentrate more on matching technique with conditions and keep fly choices to a minimum. There are diver patterns from which to choose: just look at any steelhead fly fishing book; the selection is almost limitless. Some successful B.C. patterns are the Doc Spratley, both As Specifieds, the Black Spey, the Black General Practitioner and the Eastern Canadian Atlantic Salmon Bomber.

Other fishermen will have their favorite and as long as the fly you choose complements the conditions and presentation method, it will suffice. Patterns originating south of the 49th parallel that do just as well include the Skunk, Purple Peril, Black Woolly Bugger and Grease Liner. Having confidence in a pattern increases your chances of success but to achieve consistent results you may have to abandon favorites in order to match fly pattern to conditions and presentation. Many anglers think that because the Thompson is a big river with big fish a big fly is necessary. This is false. I have caught steelhead on flies up to 5/0 and these big flies are useful to match certain conditions. Because of the desert setting and the light conditions that go with almost constant sunshine, however, to marry those conditions to the warmer water temperatures and the flat-surfaced pools of the Thompson, I rely much on my sparsely dressed flies on size 2 and 4 hooks. Following is a description of patterns that have worked well for me on the Thompson.

36

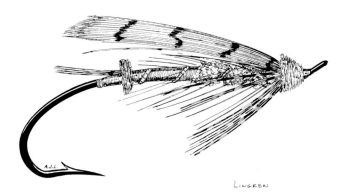

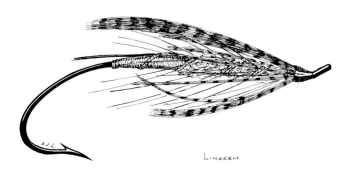

Doc Spratley

The Doc Spratley, developed in the late 1940s and popularized in the interior lakes of British Columbia by Dr. Donald Spratley, a dentist from Mt. Vernon, Washington, is such a consistent fish catcher that it is an easy fly to find confidence in. The Spratley was successfully introduced to Thompson River steelhead by Dave Winters in the late 1960s. Because of the success Winters and others have had with the Doc, it has become a staple Thompson River steelhead pattern. Winters and Wintle preferred a thin-bodied Spratley and that prompted me to change from a thick, chenille-bodied dressing to a sparsely dubbed one and because I like to offer the fish a classy fly, one tied in the classic Atlantic salmon style.

Black-, Green-, Red- or Orange-Butted Spratley

Hook: Number 4 to 1 Partridge low water
Tag: Fine, oval silver tinsel with black, fluorescent green, red or orange floss
Tail: A few fibers of Guinea fowl
Butt: Ostrich herl
Body: 1/4 black floss; 3/4 black seal fur
Rib: Medium, oval silver tinsel
Hackle: Black, one side stripped and wound from the second turn of tinsel
Throat: A couple of turns of Guinea fowl
Wing: Chinese ringneck pheasant center tail
Head: Bronze peacock herl

Later, Jerry Wintle with the help of fellow Totem Flyfisher and fly dresser Ron Grantham, made the fly very sparse which suited the clear, warm-water, early season conditions. Compared with Wintle's, my Spratley is moderately dressed.

As Specifieds

This is a fly that I developed in 1981 for summer-run steelhead, floating-line fishing. I have used it with success on a few B.C. rivers—the Morice, Thompson, Campbell and Dean, to name a few.
Hook: Number 10 to 2 Partridge low water (Number 4 and 2 for the Thompson)

Tag: Fine, oval gold tinsel with purple floss
Tail: A few fibers of purple hackle feather
Body: 1/3 purple floss; 2/3 purple seal fur
Rib: Medium, oval gold tinsel
Hackle: Black, one side stripped and wound from the second turn of tinsel
Throat: A couple of turns of teal
Wing: Bronze mallard or black squirrel tail
Head: Black celire varnish

Black Spey

Spey flies date back into the last century and originated in the River Spey Valley for Scottish Atlantic salmon. Arthur Knox, in his 1872 book, *Autumns of the Spey,* was the first to record in writing old Spey patterns and he gives the dressing for sixteen patterns. My Black Spey owes its origin to the Black Spey listed in *Autumns of the Spey.*

Hook: Number 6 to 2 Partridge Wilson
Tail: Indian crow substitute
Body: Black floss
Rib: Medium or fine gold twist, to match hook size
Hackle: Black heron or lawful substitute. For sparseness, strip one side and wind from the second turn of twist
Throat: A couple of turns of teal
Wing: Bronze mallard
Head: Black celire varnish

The long heron hackle fibers fluctuate and provide life to the Black Spey even in the slowest of currents. To steelhead, movement means something good to eat and even though returning fish are nonfeeders there is still, in some fish, that urge to test lifelike things. Steelhead are attracted to the Black Spey and it complements the floating-line technique in suitable water and light conditions.

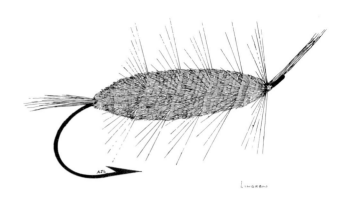

Black General Practitioner

Birthed on my tying vice in January 1984, christened with a 30 3/4 inch (78 centimetre) female steelhead on the Campbell River in February of that year, used successfully for summer- and winter-run steelhead on over two dozen British Columbian Rivers and eight other varieties of salmonids, the Black General Practitioner is my favorite steelhead pattern. The Black General Practitioner makes fishing memories. The dressing that I have simplified over the years is:

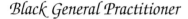

Hook: Number 2 to 5/0 Partridge low water
Tail: Black squirrel as long as the hook shank with a small golden pheasant breast feather over top
Body: Black mohair
Rib: Medium or heavy oval silver tinsel to match hook size
Hackle: Black, tied in at the tail and wound next to the oval tinsel for protection
Wing: Two black hen or spade hackles laid flat, extending just past the hook bend
Head: Black celire varnish

Bomber

This Eastern Canadian Atlantic salmon pattern adopted by steelhead fly fishermen has many variants. Thompson River regular Ehor Boyanowsky delights in catching Thompson River fish with a Bomber variation. In a recent phone call he told me about a monster Thompson River steelhead he took at one of the Totem Flyfishers' annual October outings. The fish measured by fellow Totem Flyfisher Larry Hirschkorn, was 42 inches (107 centimetres) long with a 22 inch (56 centimetres) girth—by Sturdy's formula, an impressive 27 pounds (12 kilograms). Boyanowsky's catch may be the largest fly-caught steelhead from the Thompson. I did hear of a 45 incher (114 centimetres) landed in 1993 but without a girth measurement, it is difficult to estimate an accurate weight for a fish this long.

Hook: Number 6 to 2 Partridge Wilson
Tail: Deer hair
Body: Clipped deer hair; shaped like a cigar
Hackle: Brown, palmered
Throat: A couple of turns of teal
Wing: Deer hair, extending over the hook eye

As previously mentioned, many other similar patterns work just as well as these. The dressings for the Skunk, Purple Peril, Black Woolly Bugger and Grease Liner can be found in many steelhead fishing books and I won't repeat them here. The important thing is to limit the number of flies. Three or four patterns, with some variation in size, is all one really needs to cover most Thompson River conditions and presentation techniques. You must avoid wasting time with the common change-fly syndrome and select patterns for the varying conditions and presentation methods. Keep in mind, however, that fly patterns are legion and there are no absolute rules for their use; thus, any advice must be taken at face value. I am giving you advice based on my experience, but that doesn't mean that you can't put a Doc Spratley on with a sinking line or in colder-than-recommended water or use a red pattern and catch a fish.

In general, the Doc Spratley, As Specifieds, Black Spey and Bomber best suit the floating-line and waked-fly surface presentations. The Black General Practitioner demands fishes' attention and suits the floating line for warmer water and water with a broken surface. In poor light it can be used on most pieces of water but it is not a mid-day, bright-light, floating-line pattern. The Black General Practitioner meets all my sunk-line requirements for a fly and I seldom use any other pattern for sunk-line fishing.

The Runs and Pools

THE THOMPSON IS A LARGE RIVER WITH A FLOW THAT varies considerably from year to year and, at times, from week to week and at first glance it appears that there is much water to fish. To the fly fisher, however, the immensity of the runs limits the productive pieces of fly water. But there is enough water if everyone moves along and shares.

In my earlier years on the river, I judged river height by a rock up on the Flat Run above the Rock Run. Because it broke the water surface at 1.9 metres (6 feet), this rock gave me a yardstick with which to measure other water. If the rock was showing at the start of the season, which was usually Thanksgiving weekend (early October in Canada), I considered the river to be at a reasonable height. As the river continued its normal drop through fall, more and more runs became fishable. Using the rock as a guide, however, meant that I had to fish that spot to see it. Later, Peter Blain, one of my longtime Thompson River fishing chums, told me that Water Resources had a gauge on the river downstream of Spences Bridge and that daily taped readings were available for the Fraser and Thompson Rivers by calling (604) 666-6087. The Thompson River at Spences Bridge is the last of the five recorded readings. The gauge readings and corresponding flows are in metric units. Since that time—1980—I get regular gauge readings on the river.

In different seasons, I have found I catch fish in the same spots, at the same time of the season, at the same river heights. The result of these observations is a correlation: river height to runs and fish caught. Occasionally, fishermen tell me that such-and-such a pool has changed and that although the run was good last year, it doesn't produce this season. Usually when statements like these are made, the river heights are very different. In twenty-five seasons I have noticed little change in the areas and runs that I fish. But river height can vary greatly from year to year and those who do not notice the differences in height often think that their pool has changed.

As an example, over the past twelve seasons the reading for October 10 has varied from a high of 2.6 metres (8.5 feet) to a low of 1.2 metres (4 feet). Corresponding flows of 700 cubic metres per second (25,000 cubic feet per second) and 300 cubic metres per second (11,000 cubic feet per second) show the volume of water in the river to be 2.3 times greater with the higher 2.6 metre reading. Fish moving through the system take different routes and rest in different spots with different flow regimes.

The Thompson, a big river to fly fish even at its lowest levels, presents problems for a fly fisherman, even with casts of 100 feet (30 metres), because only a fraction of the river's width can be fished effectively. Over the years that I have fished the river, I found that at a certain height in a particular run I know that the fish lie behind such-and-such rock or that the current has slowed and one can expect to catch fish there.

The first thing I do when planning a trip to the Thompson is

The Thompson is a river of memories: 9-year-old Will Houston with his November, 1975 steelhead.

Tom Brayshaw in 1936. Roderick Haig-Brown photo.

get a river height from Water Resources. With this information, my intimate knowledge of the river and my summary of how the runs fish at different heights, I can at least start my trip knowing where to fish. When strangers come to the river for the first time, they look at the vastness of the runs, scratch their heads in wonder and ask, "Where shall I start?"

I have gear-fished and fly fished the Thompson for steelhead from Epsom down to Lytton. Since 1979 I have spent most of my time fly fishing in and around the Spences Bridge area. I fish about ten runs or pools, if you wish to call them that and other minor pools if they come into shape or I can get access to them fairly easily. The runs that I regularly fish, from downstream up, are Big Horn Orchard, Graveyard, Hotel Run, Grease Hole, Y Run, Flat and Rock Run, Martel Islands and Rock Pile.

A few years ago, I went through my records and produced a chart that correlated fish caught to river height and fishing runs. When I say that the river is too high at 2.7 metres (8.8 feet), I do not mean that you can't catch fish at that height. I am saying, however, that so little of the fly water fishes well at that height that it is not worthwhile for me to drive five hours there and five hours back to spend time on the river with little fishable water. At 2.7 metres (8.8 feet) there is just about three times the volume of water to contend with over a really good fishing height of around 1.2 metres (4 feet). One of the biggest problems Thompson River fly fishermen face at any steelhead fishing height is getting on a collision path with the fish. Even when on the low side, the Thompson is still 100 to 200 metres (328 to 656 feet) wide and finding that collision path is difficult. Thompson stocks are strong swimmers and in October with an optimum migration water temperature in the mid-50s Fahrenheit (around 13°C), they have no problem moving up the middle of the river and lying way out of casting range. I recall instances of bottom-bouncing the lower Y and Grease Holes and chucking out a 2 inch (5 centimetre) hunk of 3/8 inch (1 centimetre) diameter lead as far as I could heave it with an Ambassador reel and catching fish at the extremity of the near 100-yard (90 meter) cast. The fish had found a comfortable spot to rest at that river height and if you didn't get your lure out to them, you caught nothing. Fish in holding spots like that just can't be covered by fly fishermen.

There are fishable migration routes/holding spots at all river levels.

Some runs are difficult to access by foot and a boat can be useful to move about the river. All fishing, however, has to be done from the bank. Before 1985, one could fish the river from a boat upstream of a point 1.5 kilometres (1 mile) above the Nicola River but traditionally this area was fished from the bank. During the 1984 season, some plug-pullers started to harl the river in areas previously frequented by bank anglers. Harling is a method of river trolling in which one traverses the river under power to and fro across the lies of steelhead, with lines and lures trailing behind the boat. Harling severely conflicts with bank fishing and it was necessary to put a stop to this practice or else there would be boats everywhere. I wrote a letter to the government for my fishing club, the Totem Flyfishers, and as a result the bank-only fishing boundary was extended to the upper end of the Thompson steelhead's migration—the outlet of Kamloops Lake.

Big Horn Pool

This is a small pool for the Thompson and is best fished alone or with one other person. At the most, it takes no more than an hour to fish. Located just south of the Big Horn gas station, it can be reached by traveling south on the Trans-Canada Highway. Just as you pass the Big Horn gas station and start the upgrade toward the railway overpass there is a gravel access road veering off to the right. The road leads to a parking place well above the river. From there, a good trail downstream leads to the pool. I start to fish it when the gauge hits 1.3 metres (4.2 feet). The pool is worth fishing at any height below that. It has a strong flow from the incoming chute and you need to be a strong wader to fish the upper part of this pool, especially if the river is at 1.3 metres (4.2 feet) or above. This run does have one big drawback; because it is located just above a big set of rapids most fish, when hooked, like to head for Lytton. Because there is little room to follow a fish downstream, you must use a firm hand with a hooked fish otherwise, all is lost.

Orchard Run

This is a fairly long piece of water located just north of the Big Horn gas station. Access is from the Trans-Canada Highway via a gravel road that veers off to the left from a large graveled pull-out. It takes some maneuvering to get my truck and camper around one of the bends. Once you are down the steep bank and across the usually dry side channel, however, you can drive almost to the river's edge. There is a big flat gravel bar on which to park. From

Gauge Reading (metres)	Comments
2.7	River too high.
2.5	Graveyard fishes well, Y Run tail of pool also good at this height, Martel Islands pools good.
2.3	Graveyard, Rock Run, tail of Y, tail of Grease Hole, Martel Islands pools and Car Body all worthwhile.
2.0	Graveyard, Rock Run, Martel Islands pools, Y and Grease Hole tail and Orchard fish well.
1.9	Flat starts to fish okay, Rock Run, Graveyard Orchard, Martel Islands pools all good.
1.7	Flat and Rock Run good, Graveyard okay, Piling Run right bank between bridges fishes good.
1.5	Flat and Rock Run, corner of Y coming in, Martel all good. Graveyard getting slow. Grease Hole—corner and tail, Hotel Run and Piling Run on opposite side of river are all worthwhile trying.
1.3	Y corner fishes well, Y tail coming in again with bold wading, Rock Run getting slow, Grease Hole—corner and tail, Martel Islands are all good. Big Horn Pool is wadeable and fishable.
1.0	Y corner and tail good, Grease Hole corner and tail worthwhile, all Flat good.
Less than 1.0	Much of the river becomes fishable below this height, and any likely looking spot is worth a try. I prefer the river at this height or just above for most Thompson fishing. In most years, however, the river does not drop to this height until at least November or December or not at all.

Anglers fishing the Y Pool. Fly fishing the lower Y is worthwhile only at certain river levels.

♦

there you can walk and start fishing up at the flat by the fruit tree orchard. It is a long piece of water and you can spend a fair amount of time fishing this run. It is fishable from around 2 metres (6.5 feet) on the gauge. Fish don't hold long but pass through relatively close to shore. It is one run where minimal wading is necessary. This run does have one big drawback: it is one of the spots where fishermen launch power boats and with the large camping spot on the bar, it is a popular place for other gear-type fishermen to congregate.

Graveyard Run

This is the most popular and productive fly run on the whole river. It is located opposite the native graveyard at the junction of Highway 8 (Spences Bridge to Merritt) and the Trans-Canada Highway.

There is an asphalt pull-out parking area with an historical plaque describing the great landslide of August 13, 1905. When part of Arthur's Seat Mountain on the opposite bank of the river let loose millions of tons of mud and clay came down, blocking the river. A native village was located about where the river now exists. Three native people who were fishing salmon directly under the slide were buried alive. The landslide and subsequent rise in the river killed sixteen native people. The river's flow was totally blocked for many hours and it took three weeks for the river to cut its way through the slide material. The farm across the river sits on the slide covering the old river bed. The pool we now fish was where the native village used to be. Thus, there are two reasons for calling this run the Graveyard Run: the native graveyard across the highway and the native people who were buried or drowned as a result of the great slide. From the parking spot there

is a trail down the bank and across the field to the middle of the run. This is a huge piece of water, starting at the bend in the river just south of the spectacular Murray Creek Waterfall and extending downstream for about 500 metres (1,640 feet) or close to three city blocks.

Parts of this run fish well once the river hits 2.5 metres (8 feet) and below on the gauge. The whole run fishes well from 2.5 to around 2.0 metres (8 to around 6.5 feet). Below that height, the upper part starts to fish slowly. By slow I don't mean that the fishing is poor, I mean that one waits, it seems, forever for the fly to fish around. A tactic that helps the fly fish more quickly is to allow the fly line to belly and use drag advantageously.

A person could spend the whole day fishing this run and many fishermen fish no other pool. The run seems to be a cross-over, a point in the river where the fish move from one side to the other in their upstream migration. But for a cross-over to be profitable there needs to be some good fly water above. There are few areas on the Thompson above a cross-over that are fly fishable but the Graveyard is one. A good many fish move up along the shallows of the long shingled run and fish are often taken in very shallow water along this gravel bar.

I know fishers who don't like this run because, they claim, it is boring water particularly when it drops below 2.0 metres (6.5 feet). When it gets below this height and the lower it gets, more and more of this run fishes slowly until in very low water only the bottom one third or one quarter of the run has a reasonable fishing velocity. Because I find it productive at any time during the day and at any water height, I fish this run whenever I find it is not too crowded. This is one of the easiest of Thompson runs to wade but at times, in sections of the run, deep wading is necessary. One of the special features of this run is that other than the corner at the top of the run gear fishermen usually leave it alone.

A bright 35-inch female from Martel Islands—each fly-caught steelhead is a prize won from much hard work.

The run has a slower-than-desired velocity for float or drift fishing and with no outstanding slicks to fish, gear fishermen find hang-ups much too frequently.

Across from the Graveyard Run—upstream and downstream—there are three pieces of water that can hold fish. Upstream there is the Murray Creek Run and downstream there is a big pool called the Lake Pool, easily distinguished by its name, where the top and bottom right bank can be fly fished. It is a huge, flat pool and often fish can be seen rolling throughout the tail out. Unfortunately, all too often they are out of range of the fly caster. Below the Lake Pool, and if you have a raft, the island across from the fruit stand is worth a try.

◆

The "terrors of the Thompson" are also obstacles to fish migration at certain times of year.

Hotel Run

Shortly after you leave Trans-Canada Highway and enter the part of Spences Bridge that fronts Highway 8, you will see the old Spences Bridge Hotel, now called the Steelhead Inn. Below the hotel, at most river heights during the steelhead season, you can see the pilings that supported the old bridge.

There is some good water from the pilings to just above the new Trans-Canada Highway bridge, located 400 metres (1,300 feet) downstream. The pilings are the starting point and the water is fishable from 1.5 metres (5 feet) and below on the gauge. To get

there, park alongside the highway in town and take the trail located at the old Trans-Canada Highway bridge down to the river or park about a block downriver of the hotel at the railway spur that goes over to the top of the bank. From there, walk along the spur and down the old road to the river. This old road goes through the native village located alongside the highway. Some years you can drive down to the river and some years you can't. This road goes down to a flat located along the river about 200 metres (650 feet) upstream of the highway bridge and is a launch place for one of the white water rafting companies. From there you can walk upstream to the pilings and fish down. Very little wading is necessary along this stretch. A drawback of this run is that it is popular with other gear-type fishermen and they don't move along very well.

The Grease Hole

This piece of water is located along Highway 8 just upstream of the old Trans-Canada Highway bridge. On the left, about 1 kilometre (0.6 miles) above the old bridge, is a large graveled area alongside the highway. A gravel road leads from the downstream end of this graveled area into a nicely treed camping area called the Cal Woods' Recreation Area, named after the first secretary of the Steelhead Society of British Columbia and longtime conservationist, Cal Woods.

This is a big pool but only the top and bottom of the run are worth chucking flies into. The bottom part can be fished at just about any height, but more fish seem to be caught close in when the river is on the high side and there is a good flow in the side channel abutting the highway, coaxing the fish to migrate up this route. Then again, when the river drops below 1.2 metres (4 feet), the fish are directed close in by water conditions. The corner at the head of the pool is worth a try at any time below 1.5 metres (5 feet). Grease Hole seems an odd name for a pool but if you try wading the corner without aluminum cleats and a wading staff, you will know why it is called that. Wading is necessary to fish the corner effectively because the bottom consists of large, very slippery (greasy) cobbles. Hence it is wise to wear aluminum cleats and use a wading staff. The tail of the run is much easier to wade and fish. This pool is one in which the fish can be lying so far out that you don't have a chance of covering them with a fly.

The Y Run

This run is the next one upstream of Grease Hole and is fished from the Trans-Canada Highway side of the river. It is a most popular riverside camping spot, a place where fly fishermen congregate and, as mentioned earlier, the run where Tommy Brayshaw took that first fly-caught Thompson steelhead in 1953. Access to the Y is obtained from a gravel road located just upstream of Acacia Grove Motel. The gravel access road leaves the paved road as it curves up to join the Trans-Canada Highway. The road is fairly steep and later in the season you have to be careful of snowfalls. The road can be difficult to get up and I just about got stuck there one November a few years back. At the bottom of the hill, take the road over the Canadian National Railway tracks, then the dogleg to the left along the Y branch railway spur to the treed area along the river bank. The Y railway spur gives the run its name. Because the Y Run is such a popular camping spot, with the

A 38-inch male fish taken mid-afternoon on a sun-baked glassy Graveyard Run with a #4 Green-Butted Doc Spratley.

river right there, this run gets fished more than most other runs. It is stingy to those who don't know its secrets. Like the Grease Hole, this run produces fish for fly fishermen only at certain water levels.

Like the Grease Hole corner, the Y corner starts to fish well at around 1.5 metres (5 feet) and gets better as the water drops. Bold wading is required to fish the corner properly and the same wading equipment required for the Grease Hole corner is advisable here. The bottom half of the run fishes well from 2.5 metres (8 feet) to about 1.5 metres (5 feet) then the side channel starts to get too low and the fish don't migrate up it. As a result, the fish come up the main river and tend to lie way out. The bottom part of the Y Run always looks good to fish but not much comes out of there between river heights of 1.5 to 1.2 metres (5 to 4 feet). After the river gets down to around 1.2 metres (4 feet) you can wade out quite far if you are a bold wader, even then you can only cover part of the water where fish tend to lie. The lower the river gets, the better the bottom part of the Y fishes, providing the water temperature lends itself to fish holding in the tail-out. In cold water the fish lie in the mid to upper section of the Y and, under most river heights, way out.

Flat and Rock Run

Many who fish these spots claim that they are one run. I make a distinction between them because the Flat requires deep wading over large cobbles, whereas the Rock Run can be fished from shore or by knee-deep wading. These runs are located across the river and just downstream of Nicola River. With two thirds of the Thompson stocks destined for the Nicola River, it is the major spawning stream for Thompson fish. Steelhead lie in the Thompson, upstream and downstream of the Nicola, for months before migrating up the Nicola and its tributaries to spawn.

Access to the Flat and Rock Runs is from the same road into the Y Run but instead of going over the Canadian National Railway tracks, turn left and follow the tracks upstream about 600 metres (1,970 feet) to a parking spot and turnaround. From there, it is a short walk over the tracks, upstream a short distance and down the bank to the river. If you are camped at the Y, it is a pleasant ten minute walk upstream to these runs. At the most, the Flat is about 100 metres (328 feet) long at low water and less at the higher fishing heights. It doesn't start to fish until the river gets to 1.9 metres (6 feet) on the gauge. Like many other Thompson runs, it fishes better the lower it gets. There is a break in the river's gradient at the end of the Flat where the Rock Run begins. There is not much of a distinction between these two pieces of water but I observe the distinction in my records, since I catch more fish above this break than I do below in the Rock Run. At the gradient change you wade angling to the shore, coming out just above the big submerged rock at the start of the Rock Run and carry on downstream.

The Rock Run gets its name from the many large boulders and cobbles that steelhead like to lie behind now and then. It is also referred to as John's Rock, named so by longtime Thompson River fly fishermen Jerry Wintle and Dave Winters after a local gear fisherman named John who frequented this spot. This run fishes well from about 2.3 metres (7.5 feet) and lower. It is a much smaller piece of water than the Y or the Graveyard but it is productive and worth a try anytime.

Martel Islands and Rock Pile

This spot is located about 10 kilometres (6 miles) upstream of Spences Bridge. There are three fruit farms along this section of highway from Spences Bridge to Martel. Just before the last fruit stand, the highway dips down to just above river level and Martel Islands is across the river from this farm, which incidentally was established in the 1880s by a Frenchman. Legend has it that he buried his life's earnings of several thousand dollars in a tin can somewhere in the great outdoors, so besides fishing, be on the lookout for a cache of gold. Later, after the farm had passed through two more owners, it was acquired by Joe Martel. He left two monuments to his name: the mountain behind the farm and the sign along the CN railway tracks marking the former station.

About 1 kilometre (0.6 mile) upstream of the third farm there is a very steep gravel road leading down from the Trans-Canada Highway to a parking and camping spot alongside the river. There are three pools or runs worth fishing at Martel but only one can be reached on foot from the highway side. The other two require a boat or raft, or if the river is low enough, access can be had by driving up from Spences Bridge on the dirt road on the left bank of the river. The fishable spot, called the Rock Pile, on the highway side of the river is a cobble island located about a ten minute walk downstream of the Martel parking and camping area. You can also park alongside the highway just below the fruit farm and hike along the railway tracks upstream to the island. Or park just about direct-

◆

A selection of Spratleys: Dave Winter's, top; two Wintle's, center; and author's, lower.

ly above and climb down the steep bank to the river. For good waders, the channel over to the Rock Pile can be waded at 2 metres (6.5 feet). The fishable water is about 200 metres (650 feet) long, depending on the river height. If I am fishing Martel with my motorboat, I usually don't fish the Rock Pile until later in the day. I don't think it is fair to on-foot anglers, so I leave this spot to them. Fish do not hold here long but they travel through very close to shore; thus, this run is worth a try at any height.

Martel Island has two spots—the big island and a smaller one just upstream—and they are fishable at or around 2.5 metres (8 feet). Even though the water fishes slowly in low water, these spots continue to produce fish throughout the season. During the higher levels, 1.7 to 2.5 metres (5.5 to 8 feet), one has to use a boat to get to these pools. The boat is necessary to get even between the upper and lower islands when the water heights are greater than 1.8 metres (6 feet). At river levels below 1.8 metres (6 feet), you can wade the channel between the two islands.

By crossing the river with a raft at Martel at 1.7 metres (5.5 feet) and below, the back channel can be waded along the lip of a long, slanting rapid not too far above where the back channel rejoins the main river. It is a long crossing and I wouldn't attempt it if the river is higher than 1.7 metres (5.5 feet); I prefer it lower. On one of my trips in 1988, thinking I could get across the first side channel to the smaller of the two islands, I took a raft across at Martel and hiked down to the islands. The river was at 1.7 metres (5.5 feet) and when I ventured into the main river at the top of the side channel, I found it too swift to cross. I later found in my diary that I had crossed this channel at 1.3 metres (4 feet) and have subsequently crossed it at that height. The walk downstream to the lower island was a considerable chore. I eventually did the total walk and went across to the main island along the lip of the rapids. But before I did, I tried to cross the back channel farther up, misjudged the depth and in no time found myself in water above my chest waders. I was in no danger but I got soaked and it cost me over $300 to get a new camera. To add insult to injury, I found no fish on the island that day.

A nice way to spend a day on the river is to raft from Martel to Spences Bridge and fish the Martel Islands on the way. Below Martel there are other spots that can produce fish. Again, the lower the river, the more spots become fishable. Because there are some white water sections, you should first go down with someone familiar with the river. Without stopping, the drift takes about 1 1/2 hours.

Other Spots

There are other spots upstream of Martel and downstream of Big Horn that are worth trying as well as other spots in between. Bonaparte River and Deadman Creek, up at Cache Creek and near Savona, both have runs of steelhead. Usually I am limited to the amount of time I can spend on the river and find that I can do reasonably well concentrating on the waters just described. If I had a couple of weeks or more to spend on the river, I would certainly test other waters.

The Future

I BELIEVE EVERY FLY FISHERMAN HAS A SPECIAL FLY fishing fantasy. Mine is fishing the Thompson under pristine conditions before the onslaught of civilization—with the knowledge and equipment I have now. Ian McGregor, Ministry of Environment Fisheries Branch biologist, supposes that the Thompson River—the section that steelhead frequent, Savona to Lytton and the tributaries of the Nicola, Bonaparte and Deadman Rivers—historically supported a run of about ten thousand summer-run steelhead. My arms ache just thinking about playing all those Thompson River heart-stoppers.

The Thompson is a river of dreams. Anything can happen on this river. In 1975, my nine-year-old nephew, Will Houston, fished with me on the Thompson River. You would think that starting a little fellow like Willy on a huge river like the Thompson would be difficult. It wasn't for Will; the little guy caught on fast and on his second trip he caught two fish of around 13 pounds (6 kilograms) each. How vividly I remember nine-year-old, grinning Will Houston with his two big Thompson River steelhead. Stories like Will's document the Thompson as a river of memories. The river, its fish and its fishing are precious resources to be cherished and preserved for future generations of anglers.

It will take work from the Thompson River angling community to ensure that the Thompson and its magnificent steelhead are saved. Since the settlement by Europeans, the Thompson has been assaulted by pollution from the communities upstream of the Spences Bridge fishing area. The area around Kamloops and the eastern communities are growing fast and they, like most North American towns and cities, use natural waterways to dispose of their industrial and municipal wastewater. The Thompson's size, volume of water, plus wastewater treatment are its saving grace. In addition, a good part of the watershed around the Thompson's main steelhead spawning tributaries—Nicola River and system, Deadman Creek and Bonaparte River—and the river itself are located in what is considered desert country, receiving less than 12 inches (30 centimetres) of rainfall a year and the agricultural community extracts water for irrigation, often to the detriment of rearing salmon and steelhead. Both pollution and water extraction are concerns but the Thompson's water quality remains good and is not the main threat to the extinction of Thompson River steelhead. The main culprit lies downstream: commercial and native interception of steelhead. All along its homeward journey—down the west coast of Vancouver Island, through the gauntlet of nets in the Strait of Juan de Fuca and in the Lower Fraser River—steelhead end up in the nets of these fishermen. For over a hundred years the commercial fishing industry has been taking Thompson steelhead. As the survivors of commercial and native interceptions become fewer and fewer, steelhead is still sold in fish markets. The ten thousand-strong fish run of years past has dwindled to less than 1,000 to 2,000 in recent years. Over the past fifteen years, optimum or target steelhead escapement for the whole Thompson system has never reached the desired level of 4,000. And the survey on 1991 spawners indicated a low of only 900 fish on the spawning beds. In 1992, however, the fish were allowed to swim unmolested to the Thompson and approximately 3,000 were counted in the June 1993 survey. Had the usual commercial and native fisheries' interception of two thirds of the run taken place, however, the 1992 escapement would have been similar to that of 1991. Unfortunately, for Thompson River steelhead and sport fishermen, the commercial fishing industry, native fishing and politics are closely interconnected and change comes slowly. But change must come if wild steelhead are to survive.

Over the past twenty years, the Steelhead Society of British Columbia has been the chief advocate for the Thompson River and its steelhead. Champions like Cal Woods, longtime Steelhead Society secretary; the late Eugene Rogers, Cal's successor; past president Ehor Boyanowsky; and current president Craig Orr have led the battle to protect the river, its fish and the habitat. Cal Woods spent the last twenty odd years of his life fighting for all British Columbian steelhead but his passion was for Thompson

◆

A rustic farmhouse, similar to the one my grandparents lived in when they pioneered land not too far from the Thompson River.

River stocks. For his efforts, on his death in 1986, the government dedicated the land adjacent to the Grease Hole the Cal Woods' Recreational Area. On October 27, 1990 many society members, government officials, friends of the river and members of Cal's family met at the Grease Hole to take part in the dedication ceremony and pay tribute to him.

In 1993, concerned anglers from Kamloops formed a Steelhead Society branch and that dedicated group of anglers will be working with officials of the Ministry of Environment, Fisheries Branch, the parent body of the Steelhead Society and the B.C. Federation of Fly Fishers to protect this grand sport fish so that the fly fishing aspirations of future generations can be realized by this river and its world-class, summer-run steelhead.

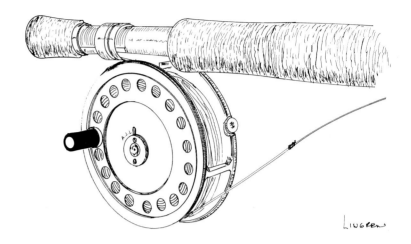

◆

The Thompson River is a challenge to the fly fisher.

If you are coming to British Columbia to fish, you should know that British Columbia has a river classification system and a guide policy. The Thompson River is in the Class II category and to fish during steelhead season requires a special permit for out-of-province fishers. Professional guiding is not permitted on the Thompson River from Savona to Lytton and there are no fly fishing shops. If you visit the Thompson you are on your own and should come prepared to search out the waters. You should also bring ample fishing equipment—rod, fly lines, flies, waders, wading staff and cleats (for treacherous, difficult wading) and a camera to catch that once-in-a-lifetime fish on film.

For information on Thompson River fishing regulations, licensing and fishing write:

> Fisheries Branch
> Ministry of Environment, Lands and Parks
> Southern Interior Region
> 1259 Dalhousie Drive
> Kamloops, British Columbia
> V2C 5Z5 Canada

For information on accommodations in Spences Bridge, the hub of Thompson River steelhead fishing, write:

> Business and Tourism Association
> P.O. Box 74
> Spences Bridge, British Columbia
> V0K 2L0 Canada

A closing thought for those planning to challenge the Thompson River: the Thompson, even with all the tips in this book, is a tough river and each fly-caught fish is an achievement. Some years ago an old gear-slinging acquaintance of mine questioned me about fly fishing for steelhead. He just couldn't see the magic I found in it. At the time, I was stumped for an answer. On reflection, however, I should have told him, "The steelhead we should prize the most are those that we have worked the hardest for." That is what each Thompson fly-caught fish is: A prize won from much hard work.